Women and Self Help Groups

WOMEN AND SELF HELP GROUPS

A Study

Dr. (Smt.) B.V.L.A. Manga

AKANSHA PUBLISHING HOUSE
NEW DELHI • GUWAHATI • VISAKHAPATNAM

AKANSHA PUBLISHING HOUSE
4649-B/21, Ansari Road
Darya Ganj, New Delhi - 110 002
Ph.: 23263193 / 9811582579 / 09435116718
Fax: 011-23263193
Email: ektabooks@yahoo.com
www.akanshapublishinghouse.com

Women and Self Help Groups: A Study

First Published 2011
ISBN 978-81-8370-292-8

PRINTED IN INDIA

Published by Akansha Publishing House, New Delhi and Printed at Harmain Offset Press, Delhi.

Contents

Preface

A recent work by Kum Kum Roy entitled *The Power of Gender and the Gender of Power* (OUP) provides an opportunity to appreciate gender related issues in all their varied dimensions and nuances observed its reviewer Padmni Swaminathan (Hindu, Book review, 25th Jan. 2011). While that being the case, my academic endeavours in the contextuality of degree earning researches were focused on marginalized to rural to urban women vis-à-vis their empowerment. What has been kindled as a little lamp to cast off that draconian poverty that subdues and subjugates the women by way of the initiatives launched by the governments and NGOs are enlightening. Hence the present study.

In the above regard it is obviously obligatory for me to gratefully acknowledge the sanction of a major research project by the UGC and also the management of Maharajah's College, Vizinanagaram need to be especially thanked for facilitating the research work.

The present work on *"Women Empowerment : Rural and Urban SHGs – A Comparative Study in Vizianagaram District"* has been divided into the following chapters.

The *First Chapter* highlights the International Conference on Women Development from 1975 Mexico to Beizing, Millennium Development Goals and Micro Credit Summit. It also gives a brief note on the Five Year Plans and their approach towards women development from the First Five Year Plan to Eleventh Five Year

Plan. It also deals with brief review of earlier studies for the period of 1997 – 2009.

The *Second Chapter* deals with the study area; rural Vs urban differentials pertaining to women; scope, importance and objectives of the study along with Research Methodology.

The *Third Chapter* deals with the Micro Finance and Self Help Movement in A.P.

The *Fourth Chapter* deals with the profile and performance of SHGs – Rural Vs Urban.

The *Fifth Chapter* deals with Social Mobilization and Income Generating Activities of Rural and Urban SHGs.

The *Sixth Chapter* deals with the Concept, Importance and Evaluation of Empowerment and how it can be a powerful tool for Poverty Alleviation.

The *Last Chapter* pertains to the Impact, Impressions and Suggestions.

Author

Abbreviations

AA	Agriculture Activities
ADB	Asian Development Bank
AH	Animal Husbandry
AIDS	Acquired Immune Deficiency Syndrome
APDPIP	Andhra Pradesh District Poverty Initiatives Project
APOs	Assistant Project Officers
APRPRP	Andhra Pradesh Rural Poverty Reduction Project
AU	Andhra University
BC	Backward Class
CGAP	Consultative Group to Assist the Poor
DDP	District Domestic Product
DRDAs	District Rural Development Agencies
DWCRA	Development of Women and Children in Rural Areas
FDP	Food Processing
FP	Forest Produce
GKY	Grama Kalyan Yojana
GOI	Government of India
GSDP	Gross State Domestic Product

HDI	Human Development Index
HDR	Human Development Report
HIV	Human Immunodeficiency Virus
ICDs	Integrated Child Development Programme
ICTS	Information and Communication Technology
IKP	Indira Kranti Pradham
IRDP	Integrated Rural Development Programme
MA	Multiple Activities
MDG	Millennium Development Goals
MDO	Mandal Development Officer
MEPMA	Mission for Elimination of Poverty in Municipal Areas
MFIs	Micro Finance Institutions
MFMI	Micro Finance Management Institution
MMR	Maternal Mortality Rate
MPCE	Monthly Per Capita Expenditure
MS	Mandal Samakhyas
MWS	Million Wells Programme
MYRADA	Mysore Resettlement And Development Agency
NABARD	National Agricultural Bank for Rural Development
NGOs	Non-Governmental Organizations
NPA	Non Performance Assets
NRY	Nehru Rojgar Yojana
NSS	National Sample Survey
OBCs	Other Backward Classes
PMIUPEP	Prime Minister Integrated Urban Poverty Eradication Programme
PRIs	Panchayat Raj Institutions

PRODEM	Foundation for the Promotion and Development of Micro Enterprizes
PRSPs	Poverty Reduction Strategy Papers
PT	Petty Trades
RRBs	Regional Rural Banks
SAPAP	South Asia Poverty Alleviation Programme
SCs	Scheduled Castes
SERP	Society for Elimination of Rural Poverty
SHGs	Self Help Groups
SHPI	Self Help Promoting Institution
SITRA	Supply of Improved Tool kits to Rural Artisans
SJGSY	Swarna Jayanthi Gram Swaraj Yojana
SJSRY	Swarna Jayanthi Shahari Rojgar Yojana
SK	Skill-oriented activities
SLF	Slum Level Federation
ST	Scheduled Tribe
TLF	Town Level Federation
TPOs	Town Project Officers
TRYSEM	Training of Rural Youth for Self Employment
UBSP	Urban Basic Services for the Poor
UN	United Nations
UNDP	United Nations Development Programme
UNESCO	United Nations Educational Social and Cultural Organization
UNIFEM	United Nations Development Fund for Women
VOs	Village Organizations
W W B	Women World Banking
WPR	Work Participation Rate

List of Tables

Map/Charts/Figures

1
Introduction

The strength of the Nation lies in the strength of its people, especially the women folk. Women represent half of the sources and half the potential in all societies. In India, women form a significant part of labour force. However, their contribution remains invisible and unrecognized women account for 90 percent of labour force in informal sector, which is neither captured in the country's population census nor accounted in the National accounts. The productive capacities of women, who constitute almost half of the population, remain unaccounted, thus reinforcing their subordinate roles. They work unceasingly from girlhood to old age, regardless of whether they are paid for the work or not-women are economically active as workers and producers and contribute significantly to the national economy, yet they have no access to a regular, stable income (Nanavaty, 2000). The lack of capital and assets, low and irregular income, aided by poor working and living conditions, low bargaining power and lack of outside linkages and opportunities for skill upgradation, all these interlinked factors drag these women into a morass of deprivation trapping them in the vicious cycle of poverty (Sinha, 2002).

In Indian conditions, poverty in general and extreme poverty in particular have a significant 'gender' dimension. Women are more sensitive than men to the extremes of poverty and its consequences. For poor households, the woman's capacity to work, her health, her knowledge and skill endowments are often the only resources to fall back on for survival. The women in India are therefore, critical to the process of moving their families out of poverty (Singh, 2005).

Micro Credit Summit Campaign's 2005 report argues that the campaign offers much needed hope for achieving millennium development goals, especially relating to poverty reduction. Till 1990s, the entire poverty alleviation programmes were quantitatively impressive but qualitatively weak.

Women bear a disproportionate burden of the world's poverty. Statistics indicate that women are more likely than men to be poor and at the risk of hunger because of the systematic discrimination they face in education, health care, employment and control of assets (Shahin Razi, 2007). Poverty implications are widespread for women, leaving many without even basic rights such as access to clean drinking water, sanitation, medical care and decent employment. According to some estimates, women represent seventy percent of the world's poor. They are often paid less than men for their work, with the average wage gap in 2008 being 17 percent. Women face persistent discrimination when they apply for credit for business or self-employment and are often concentrated in insecure, unsafe and low-wage work. Eight out of ten women workers are considered to be in vulnerable employment in South Asia, with global economic changes taking a huge toll on their livelihoods.

The current financial crisis is likely to affect women, particularly severely. The International Labour Organization estimates that the economic downturn could lead to 22 million more unemployed women in 2009 jeopardizing the gains made in the last few decades in women's employment (UNIFEM).

About one billion people in the world live in extreme poverty, defined as living on less than $ 1 per day. Seventy percent of these are women. More than 800 million go hungry each day, and two-thirds of these are women. Sociologist Diana Pearce coined the term "feminization of poverty" to describe the gendered nature of poverty. The proceedings of the first Asia Pacific Eorum on Poverty, while discussing poverty among Indian women, says "If we accept the definition of poverty as denial of choices and opportunities for a better life, then feminization of poverty is less a question of whether more men than women are poor than of severity of poverty and greater hardship women face in lifting themselves and their children". (Beijing Conference – A Platform for Action).

An UNESCO report on the feminization of poverty found the growth of female-headed households as one of the contributing factor to poverty. Worldwide women an average earn just over 50 percent of what men are earning often; women obtain low-wage work because of persistent sexual discrimination in terms of employment and wages.

Poverty is a scourge that often affects females worse than males, for it exacerbates in household inequalities in favour of males and leads to the neglect of girl children and inadequate health care for expectant mothers (Goel, 2004).

Among the disadvantaged community "India has the world's largest number of poor women" as remarked by late Mahabul Haque, U.N. Special Adviser in his Keynote address in a Seminar at Mumbai. Gender inequality is strongly associated with Human Poverty Index (HPI) value of 28.8% for India and ranks 88th among 135 countries. Gender disparity can be seen in proper perspective through the lens of Human Development Index (HDI), Gender Development Index and Gender Empowerment. The Indian ranking and value of HDI according to HDR 2009 is 0.648, Gender Development Index 0.633 and Gender Empowerment 0.451 set us thinking, that poverty may be some reason, but low Gender Development Index and poor Gender Empowerment are a clear indicative of the low status and poor position of women in our country. Now, United Nations Organization has realized that feminization of poverty is a global phenomenon and gave a call to all the countries to take more seriously, the commitment already made to give poverty reduction high priority nationally and internationally.

While debating the position of women in relation to poverty a brief review to pertaining to women development programmes and conferences held at the international level becomes imperative. The first United Nations World Conference on women which was held in Mexico City in 1975, was followed by the United Nations Decade for Women: Equality, Development and Peace (1976-85). The second conference held in Copen Hagen in 1980, adopted a programme of action for the second half of the United Nations Decade for women: Equality, Development and Peace. It was noted that due to a growing recognition of the critical importance of integrating women to national socio-economic policies and plans, there had been some progress. But due to compartmentalization of women's issues the progress has been unsatisfactory – being unequally distributed, isolated and fragmentary in nature. Impediments to effective planning and plan implementation included the lack of an adequate resource base in terms of trained personnel, finance and inappropriate data. The third UN Conference on Women held in Nairobi, Kenya, in July 1985, adopted forward looking strategies for the advancement of women. These strategies were designed to serve as guide lines for creating a new world order based on equality, development and peace. The Fourth World Conference held in Beijing in 1995 adopted the Beijing Declaration and Platform for Action. It emphasized the unacceptable conditions of poverty in which women live and the need to provide women with access to savings and credit mechanisms and institutions. It has observed that the impact of globalization resulted in increased poverty of women and the extent varies from region to region. Women contribute to the economy and to combating poverty through both remunerated and unremunerated work at home, in the community and in the work place. The empowerment of women is a critical factor in the eradication of poverty.

The Beijing Conference urged the international community, governments and society to act in a number of ways:

(1) Introduce measures to integrate or reintegrate women living in poverty and socially marginalized women into productive employment and the economic mainstream.

(2) Enhance the access of disadvantaged women, including women entrepreneurs, in rural, remote and urban areas to financial services through strengthening links between the formal Banks and intermediary lending organizations, including legislative support, training for women and institutional strengthening for intermediary institutions with a view to mobilizing capital for those institutions and increasing the availability of credit.

(3) Use credit and savings methodologies that are effective in reaching women in poverty and innovative in reducing transaction costs and redefining risk.

(4) Support institutions that meet performance standards in reaching large number of low income women through capitalization, refinancing and institutional development support in forms that foster self-sufficiency.

Micro Credit Summit (2005) essentially summarizes that "The time has come to recognize Micro credit as a powerful tool in the struggle to poverty eradication and economic independence". The first and foremost goal of the Millennium Development Goals is to reduce extreme poverty by the year 2015.

Despite the attention given to the situation of women, discrimination remains rampant, from access to education and health care, to access to and control over productive assets and to opportunities in income generations activities. Improving women's access to economic opportunities and enhancing returns on their efforts, therefore will be central to the goal of poverty eradication and the achievement of Millennium Development Goals.

In addition to reviewing the development strategy and poverty alleviation for women at the International level, an attempt is now made to examine the various programmes and policies made by Indian Government towards women development and empowerment.

Over the years the country has evolved the planning strategies on women and children, from 'welfare' to 'development' to 'empowerment'.

The approach in the First Five Year Plan (1951-56) was to provide adequate services to "promote the welfare of women". The second, third, fourth and fifth plans, including the four years of plan holiday that preceded the Fourth plan continued the same approach for the welfare of women. The concept of women's development was mainly 'welfare' oriented and was clubbed with other categories of welfare seekers such as the old and disabled. The schemes of condensed course of education for women and socio-economic programmes were introduced during the Second plan (1956-61) and that of Working Girls Hostel and Short Stay Homes in Fourth plan (1969-71). These were the only women specific programmes of the Department during the first twenty eight years of the planning history.

The end of the Fourth plan has seen the release of the monumental report of Committee on Status of Women in India entitled "Towards Equality" which revealed that the dynamics of development has adversely affected a large section of women and created new imbalances and disparities. As a consequence, A Women's Welfare and Development Bureau was set up in 1976 under the Ministry of Social Welfare to indicate necessary policies, programmes and measures for the upliftment of women. Four separate working groups on employment of women, Adult Education Programmes for women, women in Agriculture and Rural Development were setup to chalk out strategies for action in all these areas. These led to a definite shift in the approach from 'welfare' to 'development' in the Sixth plan (1980-85), which recognized women as participants of development and not merely as objects of welfare. In the Seventh plan, the basic approach has been to inculcate confidence among women and bring about an awareness of their own potential for development. An integrated multi-disciplinary approach was adopted for income generating activities and to enable women to participate activity in socio-economic development. The Seventh Five Year Plan (1985-90) continued the stress on generating both skilled and unskilled employment of women. Three landmark reports, namely Shrama Shakti, the Report of the National Commission on Self-employed Women and women in informal sector, National Perspective Plan on Women (1988-2000) and SAARC Guidebook on women in development were prepared during this period. The Department of Women and Child Development was set up in 1985 to serve as a legal point for women and children with in the national machinery.

Recognizing the role and contribution of women to development, the Eighth Plan (1990-95), adopted the strategy to ensure that 'benefits' of development from different sectors do not by pass women and special programmes are implemented to complement the general development programmes. Two new schemes, which were introduced during this period, were Mahila Samridhi Yojana and Indira Mahila Yojana. The other major developments during this plan period were setting up of a National Commission for Women and National credit fund for women known as Rashtriya Mahila Kosh, and the 73rd and 74th constitutional amendments where in one-third of seats of rural and urban self governing institutions were reserved for women. Empowerment of women being one of the primary objectives of the Ninth plan, it has directed both the Centre and States to adopt a special strategy of 'Women's Component Plan' through which not less than 30 percent of funds are earmarked in all the women related sectors and proposed a strategy of holistic approach towards empowering women. While organizing women into Self Help Groups marked the beginning for a major process of empowering women, the institution thus developed were provided a permanent forum for articulating their needs and contributing their perspectives to development.

The Tenth Five Year plan (2002-2007) had designed a three-pronged strategy of social empowerment, economic empowerment and providing for gender justice. Social empowerment is ensured by creating an enabling environment through adopting various policies and programmes for development of women, besides providing them easy and equal access to all basic minimum services. Economic empowerment ensures income generating activities with both forward and backward linkages with the ultimate objective of making all the women economically independent and self-reliant. Thirdly, gender justice eliminates all forms of gender discrimination.

The focus in the XI five year plan (2007-12) has been to buildup the capacity of SHGs realising the fact that these are in a more advantageous position to combine their resources and talents for enabling viable income generating activities, as compared to a lone individuals efforts. Many of the SHGs have developed and flourished to become trend setters and peer leaders in their region. The time has now come to consider the transformation of these SHGs which have developed considerable capacity and experience to further expand into larger community based organizations. Such organizations can operate on a bigger scale and therefore take advantage of their scale of economies to bring down costs and become more competitive in the markets; they are also in a position to shift from micro credit to larger credit facilities offered by banking institutions and thereby come into their own as a formidable economic force.

Micro credit finance

The thrust area of 11th Five Year Plan is Micro Finance. Micro credit will continue to remain the back bone of SHG finances and therefore will need to be strengthened and streamlined in the 11th plan. There have been many instances of exploitative rates of interest charged by the unscrupulous agencies which has led to economic distress in many parts of the country. Therefore, it has become imperative for the Ministry of Finance formulates regulatory mechanism for micro credit leading to make the system more transparent and beneficial. There is need to strengthen micro credit institutions to make it more pro-active and enable to play a pivotal role and nodal role in guiding credit framework for women. The efforts are being complemented by steep jump in budgetary outlays for social sectors, along with dedicated initiatives for removing poverty and increasing income generating activities. The main task of the Eleventh Five Year Plan is to ensure that women are at the centre-stage of all the activities – economic, social and political. There exists a two-way link between economic growth and poverty and gender inequality. On one level, poverty and the lack of growth exacerbated gender disparities. At another level gender inequalities undermined the prospects for poverty reduction in fundamental ways.

The rationale for economically empowering women is compelling for both for its own sake (intrinsic) and for other spill over benefits (instrumental). Research indicates that economic participation of women, their presence in the workforce in quantitative terms–is important not only for lowering the disproportionate level of poverty among women, but also as an important step towards raising household income and encouraging economic empowerment on the whole.

Amartya Sen says that societies need to see women less as passive recipients of help, and more as dynamic promoters of social transformation. The term "feminization of poverty" is often used to illustrate the fact that a substantial percentage of poor are women and that the gap between women and men in poverty has not lessened.

Women's work in India–Invisible, unrecognised and unremunerated (World Bank Report)

- India has 397 million workers.
- 123.9 million are women.
- 106 million are in rural areas.
- 18 million are in urban areas.

- Only 7% of India's labour force is in the organised sector, 93% is in the unorganized and informal sector.
- 96% of women workers are in unorganised sector.
- Female Work Participation Rate (WPR) has increased from 19.7% 1981 to 25.7% in 2001.
- In rural areas female WPR has increased from 23.1 to 31 percent.
- In urban areas it has increased from 8.3 to 11.6 percent.
- But women reported as non-workers in the census found to spending 4 hours a day picking, sowing, grazing cattle, threshing, or working as domestic servants 8 to 10 hours a day.
- ILO methodological studies indicates that major female labour-force activity rates rose radically with a wider definition of "economic activity" to cover informal sector and non-market activities from 13% to 88% in India.

Women informal workers are concentrated mainly in agriculture – so much so that three-quarters of all employed women are in informal employment are in agriculture. 90 percent of those employed in manufacturing and construction are also in unorgnized sector. Within manufacturing, they predominate in certain industries such as garments, textiles, food and electronics. The seasonality of work in this sector and the lack of other avenues of work make them vulnerable to a range of exploitive practices. Thus they remain exposed to the pangs of poverty.

At this juncture it is contextual to refer to poverty alleviation/ Income generating activities. These are important since the target for the end of the Tenth plan was to reduce poverty by 5 percent points. In these programmes it is important to focus on women as they are amidst poverty within households. The programme strategies include mobilizing and organizing the target groups, including women into Self Help Groups.

Despite various attempts in the Five year plans, poverty continues to be a stigma in the country. According to a recent Indian Government Committee constituted to estimate poverty, nearly 38% of India's populations (380) million are poor. The report is based on a new method and the figure is 10% higher than the present poverty estimate of 28.5%. The committee headed by S.D. Tendulkar has used a different methodology to reach at the current figure. It has taken into consideration indicators for health, education, sanitation; nutrition and income as per National Sample Survey of 2004-05 (*Poverty in India* – Wikipedia). Integrated Rural Development Programme launched in 1979-80 was the first major self-employment programme. Due to several operational bottlenecks, the programme did not deliver the goods to the desired extent.

The limited impact of plans and programme in the removal of poverty and employment generation, has led the Government of India to constitute a committee under the Chairmanship of S.R. Hashim to review and rationalize the various centrally sponsored schemes for poverty alleviation and employment generation (GOI, 1997). The committee noted that there had been a considerable overlap and duplication as far as the implementation of the schemes at the grass-root level was concerned. It was considered necessary to rationalize and simplify the schemes to minimize overlap so as to make them more beneficiary-friendly. As far as IRDP and the other self-employment programmes are concerned, the committee suggested that the government should make a concerted effort to move away from individual beneficiary approach to a group approach. The basic philosophy was to reduce the extent of leakages, improve the viability of the self-employment projects and provision of sustained employment to the poor.

Acting upon the recommendation of the Hashim Committee, in 1999, the GOI clubbed together employment generation programmes into four broad groups, viz. Programmes for (a) Self employment, (b) Wage employment, (c) Area development like Drought Prone Area Programme and Desert Development

Programme, (d) Minimum needs like (Indira Awas Yojana, Programmes on sanitation etc.). As far as the self-employment programme is concerned, the IRDP and its allied programmes viz. Development of Women and Children in Rural Areas (DWCRA), Training of Rural Youth for Self Employment (TRYSEM), Supply of improved Tool-kits to Rural Artisans (SITRA), Ganga Kalyan Yojana (GKY) and Million Wells Scheme (MWS) were restructured and revamped. In 1999, a single and holistic microfinance driven self employment programme, Swarnajayanthi Gram Swaraj Yojana (SGSY) was implemented after subsuming IRDP, DWCRA, SITRA, MWS and GKY. This programme is a holistic programme of micro-enterprises covering all aspects of self-employment which includes organizing rural poor in to SHGs. It aims at bringing the assisted poor families (Swarojgaris) above the poverty line by ensuring an appreciable level of income suitable over a period of time. The main tool used to achieve this objective is the organization of the rural poor in to SHGs through the process of social mobilization, training, capacity building and provision of income generating assets. It builds the self-confidence of the poor through community action, collective decision-making, prioritization of their needs and resources and improves their collective bargaining power thereby empowering them socially and economically. The implementing mechanism includes the various agencies like District Rural Development Agencies (DRDAs), Banks, Line departments, Panchayat Raj Institutions (PRIs), non-governmental organizations (NGOs) and other semi-government organizations.

The Tenth Plan (2002-07) tried to ensure effective implementation of the SGSY programme in the rural areas of the country. This programme is still under implementation in the 11th plan period (2007-12) which envisages an all inclusive growth.

Poverty elimination stratagies in urban areas

Though poverty is rampant in rural areas, the poor in India's urban and semi-urban areas also battling against the harsh reality of abject poverty and urban poverty has been on the raise due to rapid urbanization. As a result to reduce the levels of poverty with- in India's urban regions strategies have been initiated to motivate the people, creating awareness, social mobilization and organizing the urban poor into self help groups.

Attempts to reduce urban poverty in India began in the 1990s. The Urban Basic Services for the Poor (UBSP) a program under the Ministry of Urban Affairs initiated in 1992, through forming neighbourhood groups for community participation.

Swarnajayanthi Shahari Rojgar Yojana (SJSRY) in 1997 is an amalgamation of Urban Poverty alleviation programmes viz., Nehru Rojgar Yojana (NRY), Prime Minister Integrated Urban Poverty Eradication Programme (PMIUPEP) and Urban Basic Services for the Poor (UBSP). Though actions began in 1990's, efforts have not focussued on organizing people into sustainable institutions in the urban areas.

Andhra Pradesh, one of India's poorest state has used development of SHGs extensively as a primary tool of poverty alleviation and empowerment. A.P is the fifth largest state in India, with a population of 76 million of which three fourths live in the 26,500 rural villages. According to the survey of IX Five Year Plan (1997-2002) carried out by the Government of A.P, the State is among the poorest in India with many indicators below the national level. In Andhra Pradesh, the use of SHGs to rout out poverty by initiating alleviation programmes through National and State, as well as NGO efforts. The evolution goes back to 1979, with the National implementation of the Integrated Rural Development Program (IRDP) that targeted the poorest of the poor, under which as a sub-component in 1982-83, the Government of India (GOI) started the Development of Women and Children in Rural Areas program (DWCRA) in collaboration with UNICEF. Over time, DWCRA groups all over the state were strengthened.

Government initiative and sponsorship of SHGs are linked more recently to what are called the SAPAP groups. In 1996 the

South Asia Poverty Alleviation Programme (SAPAP) a pilot project was conducted in three districts of Andhra Pradesh. SAPAP was assisted by the UNDP. It emerged out of the 1993 Dhaka declaration for eradication of poverty which was the result of the need for an action plan to study the regional problems of persistent poverty, felt in 1991 where the SAARC heads of the state met at Colombo and established the independent South Asian Commission on Poverty Alleviation. The programme has covered 66,000 households, that constitute 34 percent of the total households of the project area and 64 percent of the total target group households.

Subsequent to the success of SAPAP, the processes in A.P have generated a successive upscaling of SHG promotion. The upscaling of SHGs in Andhra Pradesh has been both in terms of numbers as also in terms of structure. The Government of AP incorporated the 'Social Mobilization Approach' into its major poverty reduction project, 'Velugu' (light) comprising in the first phase of Andhra Pradesh District Poverty Initiatives Project (APDPIP), a five year project (2000-2005) being implemented in the six poorest districts in the State – Adilabad, Ananthpur, Chittoor, Mahabubnagar, Srikakulam and Vizianagaram. Given its success in the first phase, the government has rolled out the second phase of Velugu - Andhra Pradesh Rural Poverty Reduction Project (APRPRP) in the remaining 16 districts of the State. The new phase started in 2003 and is designed to last 5 years, reaching approximately 550 disadvantaged Mandals in the remaining 16 districts of the State. The total cost of the project is estimated in US$ 257.4 millions of which US$157 millions are to be spent in the Community Investment Fund only. Of the US$157 millions, 75 percent will be spent on productive activities while the remaining 25 percent will be directed towards social and infrastructure activities. The project is financed by several stakeholders: the World Bank is providing a loan for US$150 millions (54 percent of the total), the communities are investing US$13,79 millions, the Community Building / Micro-finance Institutions are providing US$51,47 millions and the Government of Andhra Pradesh is investing US$ 59,93 million. In the year 2005, the scope of the project was expanded to cover all Mandals and all villages of the state and the comprehensive programme was named as "Indira Kranthi Patham" (IKP). In this programme the activities of both rural and urban SHGs were integrated. Government of A.P. established an independent support organization in the name of "Society for Elimination of Rural Poverty" (SERP) to implement poverty elimination project which aim at social mobilization to enhance livelihoods and employment generation opportunities of the rural poor. On the same lines to implement poverty alleviation programs in urban areas, Mission for Elimination of Poverty in Municipal Areas (MEPMA) was established. Thus from the year 2005 onwards SHG movement in A.P was going in the name of IKP. The basic objective of this integration is to implement various programmes for strengthening of SHGs with similar implementation strategy. The new scheme IKP is designed by clubbing women empowerment with poverty alleviation. This is a statewide poverty reduction program to enable the poor to improve their livelihoods and quality of life through these organizations. It aims to cover all the rural and urban poor households in the state with a special focus on the 30 lakh poorest of the poor households. The program for Rural Self Help Groups is implemented by Society for Elimination of Rural Poverty (SERP), Department of Rural Development Agencies (DRDAs) at the district level. The Chief Minister of A.P. is the Chairperson of the Society.

Poverty has many dimensions changing from place to place and across the time. There are two inter related aspects of poverty– Urban and Rural Poverty. The main causes of Urban Poverty are predominantly due to impoverishment of rural peasantry that forces them to move out of villages to seek some subsistence living in the towns and cities. To eradicate poverty in urban areas, A.P. took up through the agency MEPMA (Mission for Eradication of Poverty in Urban Areas). It brings all the ongoing programs in to a single integrated project with participation of the urban poor women. It is applicable to all urban towns (seven Municipal

Corporations and 109 Municipalities in the State) on a whole town basis.

Presently under the rural program facilitated by the Society for Elimination of Rural Poverty (SERP), there are about 7,08,395 Rural SHGs (SERP, Report 2007-08) which receive support and monetary assistance from 34,269 village organizations. These village organizations in turn are supported by 1086 Mandal Samkhyas. In response to the remarkable success of the SHG model in reducing rural poverty, more than 1,75,000 SHGs have been established in 124 Municipal towns and 1,574 slum level federations have been created within 68 Municipal towns (Report of MEPMA -2008). IKP was a statewide poverty reduction project.

It is important to understand that under IKP both rural and urban SHGs through microfinance initiatives has saved on duplication and transaction costs and has also been instrumental in changing perceptions about the credit worthiness of the poor. Organizing the poor into groups has reduced the transaction costs to a very atomized demand.

IKP builds on more than a decade long, statewide women's self-help movement. The focus is on deepening the process, providing institutional structure and developing a framework for sustaining it for comprehensive poverty eradication. It is the single largest poverty reduction project in South Asia. The State of A.P. has been the focus of attention on the world map primarily due to its proactive government and the significant strides made by its SHGs.

Institutional structural building has taken the shape of forming new edifices. The project focused upon the creation of self managed grass root level institutions of the poor, such as SHGs.

The Government of A.P. has adopted a multifold strategy to eradicate poverty which is multidimensional. Eradication of poverty has been the overriding objective since the beginning of the economic plans in India. Eradication of poverty through overall economic and social development by ensuring equitable access to resources and skills as well as by widening opportunities for gainful employment to the deprived sections of the society is enumerated as the principal objectives of all the developmental programs initiated by the government. It is realized that economic growth is not enough and there is need for the intervention of the State Government to reduce poverty. Most of the poverty alleviation programs are designed by the Centre and implemented by the State on fund sharing basis for financing the programs. In order to make poverty reduction process sustainable, significant initiatives have been brought over recently to create congenial environment for poverty alleviation in terms of decentralization to strengthen Panchayat Raj institution and group approach through the formation of women SHGs. These initiatives are to ensure women's active participation in planning, implementation and post-implementation process. In this backdrop, the present study is proposed to assess the performance of rural and urban SHGs in Vizianagaram district.

Review of literature

There have been several studies since the last three decades on poverty alleviation of poor women, and Self Help Group (SHG) movement as an instrument for women empowerment. It is desirable to review the relevant literature while handling a research problem. A review of literature places a research study in its proper perspective by showing the amount of work already carried out in the related areas of study. The studies conducted in and outside the country have also reconfirmed that SHG movement has created not only awareness among women but also helped them to take up income generating activities thereby facilitating empowerment. In this chapter, it is proposed to give details of some findings related to Micro-finance, Self Help Groups, and then contribution to empowerment of women during the past one decade.

Manju Devi, K. (1997) says that a majority of rural women are from landless agricultural labourers, marginal farmers, artisans and other service castes. Most of these women belong to families below poverty line and with the families they are most disadvantaged in terms of socio-economic status. The government has recognized the need of upliftment of socio-economic status of women and priority has been given to them in the poverty alleviation programmes during different Five Year Plans. In this work, impact of IRDP on socio-economic status of rural women been studied elaborately. This study has covered the following aspects: Importance and an overview of past studies on selected field, objectives, methodology and profiles of selected districts, Mandals and various poverty alleviation programmes. The socio-economic factors, responsible for success of trade; relationship between repayment of loan and socio-economic factors of beneficiaries; impact of success of trade on living conditions, economic dependence and status of respondents and suggestions and recommendations for further improvement of implementation of the programme.

Osman (2000) states that micro-finance schemes alone cannot alleviate poverty. The battle for total eradication of poverty requires combining micro-finance schemes with parallel, complementary programmes addressing to social and cultural dimensions of want, privation, impoverishment and dispossession.

Sankaran (2004) says through urbanization in India, as in many countries is a natural process, its implications on the rural-urban divides during the reforms/decentralization period have not been addressed adequately. Similarly the rationale and scope of alternative strategies like development partnership between rural and urban sectors has also not been seriously discussed. It is highly appropriate that academics, policy makers, professionals, NGOs and the concerned public take up a serious discussion of rural-urban partnership in development and explore options in forgoing sustainable alliance between them. It is time to recognize these two as complementary to each other and strengthen rural-urban partnership.

Das (2005) studies the core objectives of rural development vis-à-vis poverty alleviation, to enhance the income level of poor women. He opines that group approach makes rural women more capable for considerable improvement in their quality of life. At this point of view, micro-financing or group lending is being looked upon as the instrument that can be considered as the golden stick for poverty alleviation vis-à-vis rural developments. SHG plays a vital role in development of group dynamics, building leadership quality to realize their potentiality and self belief. Micro-credit is an alternative source of credit for the poor women who earlier were considered as non-bankable. This system not only provides credit, most important input for development, to the poor section of the societies, but also aimed for their capacity building. The phenomenal growth of SHGs indicates that weaker sections of the society are also capable to sharpen their micro-entrepreneurial skills with the help of their own savings, and additional bank credit, as needed. At this point, micro-credit-SHG-integration could be the way out for women development and empowerment.

Purushotham (2005) examines the SHG members living in regions of high poverty, low levels of agricultural surpluses, scanty resources and underdeveloped infrastructure. In this backdrop, he develops market strategies for SHG members. He says the real constraint for micro-enterprises promotion is not shortage of funds, but the scarcity of suitable extention officers at the gross root level. Field evidence suggests, that with appropriate market support strategies, the members of SHGs could be effectively assisted to identify and build micro-enterprises as a sources of their employment and income.

Sahu and Tripathy (2005) says that seventy percent of the world poor are women. Access to poverty through banking services is important not only for poverty alleviation, but also for optimizing their contribution to the growth of regional as well as the national economy. Self Help Groups have emerged as the most vital instruments in the process of participatory development and empowerment. The rural women are marginalized groups in the society because of socio-economic constraints. They remain backward in the lower position of the social hierarchical leader. They can lift themselves from the morass of poverty and strengthen through micro-finance and formation of Self Help Groups.

Afro Asian Rural Development Organization (2006) tried to understand the concept of Self Help Groups (SHGs) and its impact on rural development and critically examined the role of governmental voluntary agencies in promoting rural entrepreneurship and developed strategies to strengthen and revitalize their role; and understood rural entrepreneurship and innovation for competitive advantage. Thus, enterprise development was considered as a powerful tool to eradicate poverty especially among rural women as they are at the lowest rung of the poverty laden in all the Afro-Asian countries. In theory, there are a number of special provisions in a country to promote women entrepreneurs, but in practice they are not implemented in totality and hence women are prevented from availing facilities meant for them. In fact, two powerful approaches to empower women and rural entrepreneurship have emerged during the last decade: formation of SHGs especially among women; and clusters among similar or mutually related enterprises. The formations of SHGs among women have fetched noticeable results in many developing countries. The SHG approach has proved successful not only in improving the economic conditions through income generation, but in creating awareness about health and hygiene, sanitation and cleanliness, environmental protection, importance of education and better response for development schemes. Similarly, cluster approach for promotion of rural enterprises has also been very effective and used in handicrafts, handlooms, forest-based enterprises and so on.

Brody, Alyson et al. (eds) (2006) are aimed at microfinance practitioners interested in learning from the experience gained by assessing social performance of MIFs. It provides an insightful account on the objectives, constraints, and methods used by practitioners to monitor social performance of microfinance institutions. The editors have identified an important information gap on how to measure and manage social performance in micro finance. The field of social performance assessment and management in microfinance is a relatively new concept that is likely to experience further progress in applied research and organizational learning in the coming years.

Cope Stake, James et al. (eds) (2006), states that most Microfinance Institutions are not set up for profit but for social missions. One needs to note that poverty is commonly defined, based on income or expenditures and, therefore, does not fully represent the multidimensional aspect of the individual, household, or other levels. He explains the poverty assessment and targeting methods used by MFIs. He discusses in detail the approaches for measuring absolute poverty. In addition, insight is provided into the constraints of MFIs in managing surveys, and analyzing data. It looks at the impact of MFIs in local financial markets and demonstrates their usefulness by identifying different market segments and evaluating progress of the groups. Finally gives suggestions of how social performance management of microfinance by MIFs themselves can be improved in future.

Hemalatha Prasad (2006) made an attempt to understand the process of Social Mobilisation of SHGs followed by different SHG promoting institutions and its impact on employment generation and empowerment among group members. It is an analytical and critical study covering 15 states in the country to understand different nuances of functioning of SHGs, group cohesiveness, conduct of various internal processes which can set a path of empowerment. The study provides deep insights in to the overall strengths and weaknesses of SHGs as effective vehicle for development and empowerment.

Jerinabi (2006) observes women as micro and small entrepreneurs have increasingly become a key target group for micro-credit programme. Providing access to micro-credit is considered a precondition for poverty alleviation, but also for women's empowerment. As poor women are increasingly recognized to be better borrowers, they are gaining the attention of regular financial institutions. But despite the proven positive impact, entrepreneurs sector in the informal sector, micro-finance is just one pool among others to address the multiple causes of poverty, unemployment and social exclusion.

Dr. Rangarajan, C. in his *"Micro Finance and its Future Directions* (2006), outline the evolution of SHG through Micro Finance evolving through three stages. In the first stage to meet survival requirement need, in the second stage is to meet the subsistence level through investing in traditional activities and in the final stage by setting up of enterprises for sustainable income generation."

Subrahmanyam (2006) analyses the various dimensions of SHGs supported through micro-finance in East Godavari District, Andhra Pradesh, India. The study runs across various academic and pragmatic issues and present a range of government planned efforts for the economic empowerment of women. It also identifies the factors that have contributed to the performance and achievements of group strategy.

Mallick (2007), says social mobilization is an approach that empowers women to participate actively in development process through their own local initiatives and through well-informed and constructive dialogue at policy level. It is an essential tool for mobilising and engaging isolated, passive and poor women of society.

Agarwal (2008), states that poverty is a multifaceted concept. It is not just about economic deprivation. Circumstances dictate the extent to which Micro Finance Institutions go beyond the delivery of economic services in order to address the root causes of poverty in communities where they work. Microfinance may not be a panacea for poverty but is a component to fight against poverty. The services that MFIs bringing to the poor households can make a significant differences to economic welfare and the capacity for self reliance.

Ahmed (2008), evaluates the progress of micro-financing through SHG-Bank linkage programme of NABARD and its impact on the empowerment of women and reduction of poverty in India. He suggests that India should also setup a National Micro Finance Bank of India on the pattern of Bangladesh as early as possible and all the RRBs should be merged in this bank. This new bank may be quite successful in empowering women through micro-credit and eradication of poverty for the country. Poor women SHGs would be able to make investment in non-farm business activities and income generating assets and will be able to pay the amount of interest with principal in easy installment out of the profit. Thus in this manner poor women, both urban and rural, will be empowered, economically, socially, educationally and politically, through micro-financing schemes.

George (2008) in his article on Micro-finance issues and strategies states that the banking sector is not able to meet the entire credit needs of the poor and it is necessary to encourage the growth of Micro-finance Institutions, subject to appropriate regulation. It has been demonstrated that group lending ensures high rate of repayment as the other members of the group act as catalysts for repayment of loans. The SHGs also act as a form of 'Social Collateral'. Linking the SHGs to the banks has thus become a workable way of channelising micro-credit to the poor women. As the moneylenders are still dominant in the rural credit sector, it is pragmatic to institutionalize them with adequate safeguards to prevent exploitation of poor. There is also a need to shift the focus from the quantity of credit to quality of credit. In order to achieve this, emphasis should be given to SHG formation and group lending rather than individual lending. Micro-finance ombudsmen may be set up at district levels to decide on complaints regarding exploitative and illegal practices by the lenders.

Narasimha Raju (2008) says that in SHGs, collective action and solidarity is an important empowering mechanism. Collective action implies cohesion of group. Cohesion enables the member of the group to perceive common interests and act collectively. The strategy of SHGs is to create empowerment opportunities for women below the poverty line. The empowerment strategy work with poorest and most oppressed women of a selected region, urban or rural; Train activists/ change agents who are gender aware and conscious about economic programmes to interact with, mobilize learn from and raise the consciousness of such women.

The empowerment of women through SHGs would lead to benefits not only to the individual women but also the family and community as a whole through collective action for development. The empowerment of women covers both individual and collective transformation. It strengthens their innate ability through acquiring knowledge, power and experience.

Satpathy (2008) describes his field work experiences on SHGs, Micro-finance and Technology in the Indian States of Orissa, Rajasthan and Haryana. Women's empowerment is not a one-time affair but a continuous process. The impetus may arise out of experience, disadvantage or discrimination, or an aspiration to become self-dependent. The empowerment process may be based on an institutional framework and sustain through input-output exercises. Initial activities may include micro-finance, income generation, community education, information, mutual support services and advocacy. Micro-Institutions, which may be in the form of SHGs, community interest groups or co-operatives are formed and managed by the people, who have felt disadvantaged in social, economic or cultural spheres. Such institutions are owned and managed by the members democratically. There may, however, be external stimuli that help the group form, consolidate and operate.

Shylendra (2008) in his study on Role of Self Help Groups opines, though SHGs have begun to contribute in improving the economic conditions of the poor, the impact does not seem to be uniform. A foremost impact discernible is the reduced dependence of SHG households on informal sources of credit. Given the wide-spread gender bias against women in various fields, the author argues that interventions like micro-finance have the potential to enhance women's capabilities which can make a significant difference to overall development of women. The constraints and challenges facing the SHG programme to contribute more effectively for poverty alleviation and empowerment was discussed. He gave a brief note on restrictive policies of formal agencies and calls for adopting highly proactive and innovative policies to deal with SHGs. He states that the performance of SHGs to a great extent depends upon their quality of governance, management and leadership. There is a major onus on all actors involved in SHG promotion and development to further intensify their efforts in enabling SHGs to reach a mature stage.

Swarna Sadasivam, Vepa (2008) in her article discuss the instances of technology and micro-finance for the success of micro-enterprises run by rural women in India. Where extensive services are effective, women have no difficulty in mastering technologies in crop as well as no-crop enterprises. The major hurdle in the success of micro-enterprises seems to be the sustainability of the enterprises. Lack of an assured market, lack of quality control and lack of competitiveness are the major problems. Micro-finance plays a crucial role in promoting micro-enterprises. Credit is available; however profitability and assured market pose bigger problems for women than technology adoption and availabilities of micro-finance. The major hurdles are extension services, access to resources, managerial skills, quality assurance etc. These are basic problems of all micro-enterprises promoted for women in poverty groups. They need gender sensitive approaches to reach out to women.

Yerram Raju (2008) in his article Micro Finance Development and Regulation objectively examined the content of the Micro Finance Sector Development and Regulation Bill. He says that NABARD is a already operating Micro Finance Development and Equity Fund. He argues that there is no evidence at least on record that the organizations that received this type of assistance are better off than others in the conduct of their affairs. He says that there are institutional maladies and systemic failures. These need to be carefully analyzed appropriately tackled. SHGs in micro-finance sphere require being distinguished on several fronts: SHGs with consistently good performance; SHGs inadequately performing, SHGs badly performing and some medium SHGs who are entering new areas with confidence deserving encouragement. He recommends creating a separate window for supervision of Micro Finance activity in the RBI Fortress.

Berik, Günseli and Vander, Yana, (2009) examines the inter-group connectivity and micro-economic outcomes, considering various changes through which gender, growth and development interact. It upholds the salience not only of equity in opportunities but also equity in outcomes. The contribution argues that inequalities based on gender, race, ethnicity, and class undermine the ability to provision and capabilities, and examines the macro economic policies that are likely to promote broadly shared development.

It explores how the macro economy acts as a structure of constraint in achieving gender equality and in turn how gender relations in areas like education and wage gaps can have macro level impacts. Further, it underscores that the interaction of the macro economy and gender relations depends on the structure of the economy, the nature of job segregation, the particular measure of gender inequality. Finally, it outlines the policies for promoting gender equality as both an intrinsic goal and step towards improving well-being.

Elson, Diane's (2009) contribution examines how gender equality features in the World Bank's World Development Report 2006: Equity and developing focusing on its conceptual framework, use of empirical evidence, and policy recommendations. It concludes that despite acknowledging that liberalization and privatization have been captured by elites for their own benefit, the report still clings to a neo-classical understanding of how markets and competition works. Moreover, although the report emphasizes gender inequalities in opportunities as a trap that hinders economic growth, it shows no understanding of economic growth as a gender process in which old forms of gender inequality are weakened but new forms of gender inequality emerge.

Christabell (2009) in her study assesses the role of Micro-finance in building up economic and democratic capacity of women and there by enhancing their empowerment in India, with special reference to the state of Kerala. Evaluating the performance of SHGs, it tries to identify the factors. that contribute to their successful performance and sustainability. It also studies the level of participation of women in SHG and examines the group dynamics that influence their participation. The extent of participation of the poor women in the micro-finance institutions has been analyzed as well.

Patil, D.A. and Dhere, A.M (2009) explains the role of Information and Communication Technologies (ICTs) as a tool for development and the millennium declaration adopted in 2000 underscored the urgency of ensuring that the benefits of new technologies, especially ICTs are made available to all. ICTs can be a powerful catalyst for political and social empowerment of women and the promotion of gender equality (United Nations 2005:3). It examines some ICT based initiatives to empower rural and deprived women. It tries to clarify theoretical dilemma between meaning and measurement of empowerment. Finally, it focuses on the two fold need to address some of the social and technological challenges as well as policy suggested to use ICTs proactively and effectively to promote gender equality for empowerment of rural and deprived women. The study used observations, focus group discussions and review of documents to collect secondary and primary data.

2

Study Area and Methodology

The successful implementation of any development programme emphasizes the need for considering the resource base of a particular area. As this programme is a comparative study of rural and urban women SHGs, with special reference to poverty eradication, to improve their livelihood and quality of life through building their own institutions, an attempt is made to examine the poverty ratio, demographic profile at the national, state and the local levels. This chapter briefly deals with the related aspects of India, Andhra Pradesh, and the District i.e., Rural Mandals and Urban Municipalities of Vizianagaram. This chapter is divided into 2 sections. Section – I consists of demographic profile and Section – II refers to the research methodology.

Women are vital and productive workers in India's economy. They make up one third of the labour force though a 'statistical purdah' imposed by existing methods of measuring of labour renders much of their work invisible (World Bank Report 2001). Women's poverty is directly related to the absence of economic opportunities and autonomy, lack of amenities to economic resources, including credit, land ownership and inheritance, lack of access to education, support services and their minimum participation in decision-making. Poverty in urban and semi-urban areas is more acute while it is further deplorable in the rural areas.

The latest NSS (National Sample Survey) for 2004-05 is fully comparable to the surveys before 1999-2000 and shows poverty at 28.3 percent in rural areas, 25.7 percent in urban areas and 27.5 percent for the country as a whole, using uniform Recall Period Consumption. One third of world's poor are Indians. Even after more than 60 years of Independence, India still has the world's largest number of poor in a single country of its nearly 1 billion inhabitants. An estimated 260.3 million are below the poverty line, of which 193.2 million are in rural areas and 67.1 million are in urban areas. Poverty level is not uniform across India. A.P State specific poverty line in 2004-05 for rural areas is 292.95 and for urban areas 542.89.

The latest Income-criteria adopted to determine the poverty line in India is based on 2004-05 data, where it is stated that All India Level minimum income for rural and urban areas for a person per month should be Rs.356.30 and 558.60 respectively.

Sex ratio for females per thousand males at National level is 933. In rural areas it is 946/1000 and in urban areas it is 940/1000. If we examine the rural-urban distribution, rural population is 72.2 percent and urban population is 27.8 percent. At the National level, total literacy rate is 64.8 percent. Male literacy is 75.3 percent and female literacy is 53.7 percent. Again total rural literacy rate is 58.7 percent. Rural literacy rate for males is 70.7 percent and females is 46.1 percent. Total urban literacy is 79.9 percent at the National level. The urban male literacy rate is 86.3 percent and female is 72.1 percent. The work participation overall is 39.1 percent–the male work participation rate 51.7 percent and females is 25.6 percent.

India remains at an abysmal rank in UN Human Development Index. India is at 132nd place in 2007-08 as per U.N. HDI Index. It is the lowest rank for the country in over 10 years. In 1992, India was at 122nd place in the same Index.

Coming to the State level, A.P is the first largest state in the country both in terms of area and population. It has an area of

2.75 lakh sq. kms, forming 8.37 percent of the total geographical area of the country. The State population according to the 2001 census is 7.62 crores which constitutes 7.41 percent of All India Population. The total number of districts in A.P. are 23. A.P ranks 22nd among 28 states in the country and stands last among the southern states. While official estimates show that poverty in A.P rural is 11.05 percent and urban is 26.63 percent, alternative estimates reverse these ratios and place the percentage of poor yet 26.2. Given the distribution of population between rural and urban areas, the number of poor in rural areas is far more numerous than in urban areas. Availability and quality of employment, in terms, principally of wage earnings depends on skill endowment of the labour force. Literacy is the first level of skill. Literacy levels in the rural areas are lower than in the urban. The National Sample Survey reports that in 1999-2000 per thousand persons aged 15 and above, 578 were illiterate, 352 educated upto the upper primary level and only 71 educated upto secondary and above in rural areas. In urban areas the distribution was 318, 421 and 261, showing rural labour in distinct disadvantage.

This study examines the issues of inclusiveness in terms of the changes in relative positions of rural population versus urban, females versus males in health, levels of living, literacy rates and inequalities in income distribution. The following tables are demonstrative of such an rural-urban discrepancies.

Table 2.1
Rural and urban differentials, levels of living

Item	*1987-88*		*1999-2000*	
	Rural	*Urban*	*Rural*	*Urban*
Average MPCE (Rs)	160	230	454	774
Food Expenditure (%)	59	53	61	47
Percentage of poor (Official)	21.0	41.1	11.1	26.6
Percentage of poor (Deaton)	35.0	23.4	26.2	10.8

Source: National Sample Survey

Table 2.2
Rural urban differentials

Item	*Rural*	*Urban*
Birth rate	21	19
Death rate	9	5
Infant Mortality Rate	67	33
Percentage children receiving all vaccinations	54	73
Percentage of women with bmi < 18.5	43.2	19.7
Percentage of children severely underweight	2.1	0.4

Source: SRS and National Family Health Survey.

Table 2.3
Ratio of the MPCE of bottom 30 percent and top 30 percent

Year / Location	*Average MPCE of*		*Ratio*
	Bottom 30%	*Top 30%*	
1993-94RuralUrban	164202	445705	2.713.49
1999-2000RuralUrban	168221	435819	2.593.71

Source: National Sample Survey.

Health and education conditions in rural areas suffer similarly by comparison with urban areas. While birth rates in urban areas have declined to urban levels, death rates are far higher in urban areas than in the urban. Infant mortality rates in rural areas are twice those in the urban.

If we examine the work participation rates, the total number of workers is 39.1 percent. Male workers is 51.7 percent and female workers is 25.6 percent. The main workers consists of 30.4 percent, males is 45.1 percent and female is 14.7 percent. The total number of marginal workers is 8.7 percent. Marginal male workers is 6.6 percent and females is 11 percent.

Table 2.4
Literacy rates

Nation	*State*	*Type*	*Literacy*	*Males*	*Females*
India	A.P.	Total	64.8%	75.3%	53.7%
		Rural	58.7%	70.7%	46%
		Urban	79.9%	86.3%	72.9%

Source: National Sample Survey

In literacy, A.P ranks 24th among 32 States in respect of literacy in 2001. The NSS reports, that in 1999-2000, women illiterates were one and half times than the men illiterates in both rural and urban areas, explaining why women do not achieve desired employment. More women than men are engaged in casual labour (54 Vs 44 percent in rural areas and 32 Vs 22 percent in urban areas). This source also report that regular employment is held by 28.5 percent of women against 42 percent of men in urban areas, in rural areas it is 3.5 Vs 7.6. The NSS also reports that there are fewer self employed women than men in both areas.

Table 2.5
Basic information National Human Development Report, Planning Commission, India

S.No	*Indices*	*India*	*A.P*
1	Human Development Index value (2001)	0.472	0.416
2	Human Poverty Index Rank	39.36	39.78
3	Sex Ratio (2001)	933	978
4	Percentage of female in labour force 1999-2000	39	54
5	Percentage of population below poverty line 199-2000	26	16
6	Literacy rate (2001) %	65	61
7	Male literacy rate (2001) %	76	71
8	Female literacy rate (2001) %	54	51
9	Rural literacy rate (2001) %	59	55
10	Rural male literacy rate (2001) %	71	66
11	Rural female literacy rate (2001) %	47	44
12	Urban literacy rate (2001) %	80	76
13	Urban male literacy rate (2001) %	86	83
14	Urban female literacy rate (2001) %	73	69

Source: Indices – Government of India – 2001

The decennial censuses conducted in India suggest that there has been an almost monotonic decline in the sex ratio in India. In 1901, the sex ratio was 972 for every thousand males, by 1991 it had reached the lowest point at 927. In census 2001, the sex ratio increased by six points to 933. The sex rations in A.P was also showing declining trend since 1951 till 1991. However, for the first time sex ratio has increased from 972 in 1991 to 978. The sex ratio in A.P. is higher than the all India figure, which is 933. The position of A.P. is third among the four Southern states. The declining trend in sex ratio is primarily the consequence of high levels of female mortality which begins at birth, after birth or even before birth. Vizianagaram District particularly represents a varied picture of female to male ratio for various socioeconomic reasons. According to 2001 census female (1009) to male (1000) ratio is the highest in Vizianagaram District, where they out-number men. In spite of its economic backwardness it shows progress in terms of gender development. Thus there is no positive correlation between economic progress and gender development. Female literacy rate in A.P. is always low when compared to male literacy rate. According to 2001 census the make literacy rate is 70.85 as against the female literacy rate of 51.17. It is to be noticed that the female literacy rate was never equal to male literacy rate, which clearly indicates gender inequalities. Further, rural-urban and caste-wise variation can be noticed in regard to female literacy. In 2001, in AP rural female literacy was 44.36 percent while it was 69.34 percent in urban areas. Moreover SC female literacy rate in rural areas is as low as 43.35 percent and it is 34.79 percent for S.T. women. In totality the literacy rate of A.P is lower than the All India Literacy Rate and difference in literacy rate between rural and urban and between male and female is very wide.

Vizianagaram District is one of the Northern Coastal Districts of Andhra Pradesh, India. Vizianagaram town is the District Head-quarters. The District is bounded on the East by Srikakulam District, on the Southwest by Visakhapatnam District on the

Southeast by the Bay of Bengal, and on the Northwest by Orissa State. Vizianagaram district was formed on June 1st 1979, with parts carved out from the neighbouring districts of Srikakulam and Visakhapatnam. The district is named after the princely State of Vizianagaram.

Geography

It is situated within the geographical co-ordinates of 17-15' and 19-15' of northern latitudes 83-00' and 83-45' of the eastern longitudes. The district can be divided into two distinct natural divisions i.e., plains and hilly regions. The hilly agency area covers Pachipenta and Gummalakshmipuram Mandals fully and Salur, Makkuva, Rambhadrapuram, Parvathipuram and Komarada Mandals partly. Rest of the agency region mostly consists of hills covered by the Eastern Ghats, which run parallel to the coast from the Northeast to Southwest. About 51.1 percent of the land area is sown for agriculture and another 12.3 percent land is put to non-agricultural uses. The forest covers about 17.8 percent of the land about 12.3 percent of the land is barren and uncultivable. The climate of Vizianagaram district is characterized by high humidity nearly all-round the year with oppressive summer and good seasonal rainfall. There is a coast line of 28 kms in the district on the east facing Bay of Bengal. There are 8 villages and 16 hamlets consisting of 6,993 fishermen. They are situated at Pusapatirega and Bhogapuram Mandals.

It is predominantly an agriculture district, as 68.4 percent of the workers engaged in agriculture and about 82 percent of the population living in rural areas are depending on agriculture for their livelihood. There are two Revenue Divisions, 34 Mandals, 928 Panchayats and 1551 Revenue villages in Vizianagaram district. The Revenue divisions are Vizianagaram revenue division and Parvathipuram revenue division.

The District had a population of 22,49,254 as per 2001 census. They consists of 11,19,541 males and 11,29,713 females. There are 1009 females per 1000 males in the district. The total area is 6,539 sq. kms. The population density is 344 persons per km. The increase in the population during the decennium from 1991 to

2001 is 6.55 percent for the District as against 14.6 percent for the AP State. The Scheduled Caste population is 10.58 percent and Scheduled Tribe population is 9.55 percent respectively to the total population of the district. The rural population of district is 18.37 lakh which comes to 82 percent of the total population. Vizianagaram district has been comparatively backward in the field of education. The literacy rate is 51.82 percent as against the average of 61.55 percent for the entire AP State.

Table 2.6

Facts and figures–Vizianagaram District (2002-03)

Total area	*6539 sq.km*
Total population in lakhs	22,48,254
Male population in lakhs	11,19,541
Female population in lakhs	11,29,713
Percentage of SC population	10.58
Percentage of ST population	9.55
Rural population	18,36,859
Urban population	412395
Females per thousand males	1009
Scheduled Castes	2.38 lakhs
Scheduled Tribes	2.15 lakhs
Workers	9.12 lakhs
Agriculture labour	2.90 lakhs
Cultivators	3.02 lakhs
Total Villages	1551
Total No. of Towns	12
Total No. of Gram Panchayats	928
No. of Municipalities	04
Density of population per sq.km.	343
Total No. of Revenue Mandals	34
Total literacy rate	51.82
Female literacy rate	40.73
Male literacy rate	63.00
Total No. of Rural Women SHGs	29,888
Total No. of Urban Women SHGs	5,282

Source: Directorate of Economics and Statistics, Hyderabad. Chief Planning Officer, Vizianagaram (*Handbook of Statistics*, Vizianagaram district 2007-08).

Demographic Profile of Vizianagaram – Urban

According to 2001 census, Vizianagaram district is divided into 4 municipalities. Vizianagaram municipality comes under Class – I town, Bobbili municipality under Class – II, Parvitipuram and Salur are classified as Class – III towns.

Vizianagaram Municipality

Of its total population of 1,95,801, males constituents 49 percent and female constituents 51 percent. It has an average literacy rate of 68% higher than the National average of 59.5%. Male literacy rate is 75 percent and female literacy rate is 62%. In Vizianagaram Municipality 10 percent of the population is below 6 years of age. It is one of the fast growing municipalities in Andhra Pradesh.

Bobbili Municipality

It is a town, Mandal Headquarter and a Municipality in Vizianagaram district. It is located at 18.5667^{0}N, 83.3667^{0}E. It has an average elevation of 103 meters (337 feet). As of 2001 Indian census, Bobbili had a population of 50,140. Males constitute 50 percent and female constitutes 50%. It has an average literacy rate of 64 percent higher than the national average of 59.5 percent; with male literacy 71 percent and female literacy 56 percent and 11 percent of the population is below 6 years of age.

Pavathipuram Municipality

It is a town, Municipality and Revenue division in Vizianagaram district. It is located at 18^{0}46' N, 83^{0}25' E. It has an average elevation of 120 meters. According to 2001 census, it had a population of 49,692. Males constitute 50 percent and females 50 percent. It has an average literacy rate of 66 percent, higher than the National Average of 59.5 percent; male literacy is 75 percent and female literacy is 57 percent. In Parvathipuram, 12 percent of the population is below 6 years of age.

Salur Municipality

It is Municipality and Mandal Headquarters in Vizianagaram

district. It is a gateway to reach Southern districts of Orissa, Madhya Pradesh and Chattisgarh by road on the National Highway 43. It is situated at a distance of 55 kms away from Vizianagaram and 95 kms from Visakhapatnam.

It is a grade – III municipality. The extent area is 19.55 sq. miles. It is located on the banks of the river Vegavathi at 18.5333^{0}N, 83.2167^{0}E. It has an average elevation of 118 meters.

As of 2001 Indian Census, it had a population of 48,362. Males constitute 49 percent of the population and female 51 percent. It has an average literacy rate of 59 percent, lower than the national average of 59.5 percent; male literacy rate is 68 percent and female literacy rate is 49 percent. In Salur, 12 percent of the population is below 6 years of age.

The Central Government has identified Vizianagaram district as one of the poor and backward districts of Coastal Andhra Pradesh. In the coastal area from Nellore to Srikakulam, 9 districts were located and out of these 9 districts, Vizianagaram is listed among the backward areas. It is the 23rd district in the state and it is backward in all arenas. Literacy rate is lower which is less than the average of state, lack of facilities from agricultural cultivation, low infrastructure facilities and with no strategy adopted for establishing industries are responsible for the low per capita income. While the per capita income of the state on an average is Rs.35,060, the district average per capita income is Rs.25,498. Even in Human Development Index measuring also Vizinagaram is very backward. The research group recently studied the socio-economic condition of Vizianagaram revealed that the people living in poverty are 56.1 percent and poorest of the poor among them are 18.6 percent. These indices may be used as parameters for recognizing Vizianagaram district as backward district. The literacy rate is 51.07 percent and as such is lagging much behind the average of the state. It occupies 22nd place in the state. For past 4 decades, there is no change in the literacy rate. Though certain projects like Sarva Siksha Abhiyan were introduced exclusively for women, the literacy rate of women was not increased. Most of the people's representatives also belong to the category of managing the things with thumb impression only. Child labour is also recorded at the optimum level. Due to poverty, everyone in the house has to go for work. As a result of acute poverty, children who need to go to schools are going to work along with parents. Vizianagaram district is notorious for its diseases like elephantiasis and Malaria. Lands with water facility for cultivation are abysmal. The cultivated land in Vizianagaram district approximately is 2.89 lakh hectares, out of which 1.75 lakh hectares are rain-fed areas only. Rains are uneven in the seasons as a consequence of which there is disparity in produce and area for cultivation.

In 1991, the farmers are 3.68 lakh and this figure is declined to 3.22 lakh by 2001. In 1991, the agricultural labours were 3.28 lakh and by 2001 it was increased to 4,70,000. Ninety percent of the farmers are reduced to the position of agriculture labourers.

In the district the rural and industrial employability has declined remarkably. When compared to rural and industrial employability, unorganized sector is growing rapidly. There is no improvement in the standard of living but there is a large gulf both in rural and urban areas leading to regional imbalances. Industrial growth centre were started 16 years ago, but the benefits were not percolated to the people at the grass root level.

From the above study it may be understood that diversities and inequalities are discernible in almost all types of physical and cultural phenomena at various spatial scales ranging from global to local. They also distinguish themselves as urban and rural. Rural, urban differences get revealed in occupation, size of the community, density of population, heterogeneity, social differentiations, mobility, and system of interaction.

For inclusive growth, there is a need to reduce rural, urban and regional disparities and provide equity in terms of empowerment to the poor especially the women who constitute significant proportion of poor.

While average growth rate of Gross State Domestic Product (GSDP) of A.P. during 2003-07 has 7.8 percent, the District Domestic Product (DDP) and per cepita showed lower growth than that of State average.

In Vizianagaram district, exclusion continued in terms of low agriculture growth, low quality employment growth, inadequate development of women and children, concentration of poverty and low human development both geographically and in terms of social categories, increase in rural-urban disparities (Dev., 2006). To overcome regional disparities, rural-urban divide and poverty eradication, Government of A.P. has chosen Self Help Group movement under the project Indira Kranthi Patham to enhance the assets, capabilities and abilities of the poor to deal with shocks and risks. In this background, women empowerment model IKP is of high value, and the present study is conducted to evaluate the contribution of rural and urban Women SHGs towards decline in poverty and inequality, social mobilization and expansion of economic resources at the house hold level.

Scope of the study

The study is important for research in the field of rural as well as urban women empowerment. The study would provide a framework for drawing suitable programmes for women's emancipation and empowerment. The opportunities for creation of supplementary sources of income would also be explored. In short, the study would be highly useful to researchers.

This case study evaluates SHGs and the federation both in rural and urban areas, as facilitated under the project. The study is based on the field visits to the project towns and Mandals during September to December 2008, and was updated during August 2010. It integrates secondary sources of information.

Importance of the study

In the background of the above international, national and state level initiatives, it may be understood that, poverty is the root cause of all evils for development and empowerment of women. Majority of the third world women are involved in the informal sector of economic activities in which they are disproportional represented among the poorest of the poor. Yet most of these informal activities do not yield sufficient income to extricate women out of poverty. As the majority of the women do not own capital or tools and equipments of their trade, they remain vulnerable in the clutches of private moneylenders. Indebtedness puts them in a weak bargaining position with the middlemen and traders on whom they are dependent for their livelihood. Because of higher interest payment, low incomes and insecurity of work opportunities, they were caught in the persistent debt trap. At this juncture, what is needed is to develop a mechanism to improve the income generating activities and providing finance at reasonable rates on regular basis in informal sector.

The mechanism is to form these women into Self Help Groups (SHGs) and providing small loans (Micro-credit) to help them engage in productive activities or grow their tiny businesses. The main focus is not only to provide credit but also to integrate these women with other developmental activities. It was in this context Micro-finance institutions and programmes emerged around the globe and paved the way for the betterment of the women. The Government of India, while launching poverty alleviation programs emphasized the need for formation of women SHGs by mobilizing, concretizing and organizing them through a participatory process. It was in this background, the idea of micro-finance emerged in India. The operation of SHGs are based on the principle of revolving of the member's own savings. External financial assistance augments the resources available to the group-operated revolving fund. Savings precede borrowing by the member.

SHGs of women in India have been recognized as on effective strategy for the empowerment of women in rural as well as urban areas bringing them together from all spheres of life to fight for their rights. The access to credit can be seen as the motivational factor behind the formation of SHGs and the bond that sustains the groups overtime. Once a group has been formed, the credit link is established and the group meets on a regular basis and gradually the groups tend to take on much wider social role along with income generating activities. The basic idea of micro-finance is that the poor women are ready and are willing to pull themselves out of poverty if given access to economic inputs.

Objectives of the study

The researcher has undertaken this study, in order to know the performance of rural and urban women SHGs in Vizianagaram district and to ascertain the impact of micro credit on empowering women SHGs.

The major objective of enquiry is to compare and understand the rural and urban SHGs with reference to the micro-finance, mobilization of savings, utilization of micro-credit and organization, management and performance of income generating activities. It also tried to assess the role played by micro-finance in building up democratic capacity building of women and thereby enhancing empowerment. The study was intended to evaluate the performance of SHGs to identify the factors which contribute to their successful performance and sustainability. It is a holistic study which not only focuses on the SHGs and its members, but also on the role of Self Help Promoting Institutions. More importantly the study also attempts to assess the levels of empowerment as well as the potential for generating social capital among the rural and urban women SHGs. It also understands the process of group formats and impact on employment and empowerment.

Specific objectives

- To compare and evaluate the functioning of women SHGs at the rural and urban areas.
- To identify the strong, self reliant, pro-active, sustainable groups.
- To examine how SHGs act as means of poverty alleviation.
- To examine how efficiently micro-finance management system is provided to rural and urban women SHGs.
- To scrutinize various issues in the operation of rural and urban women SHGs.
- To identify the efficient management factor that influence success.

- To assess the strength and weakness of rural and urban women SHGs.

VIZIANAGARAM DISTRICT

ADMINISTRATIVE DIVISIONS

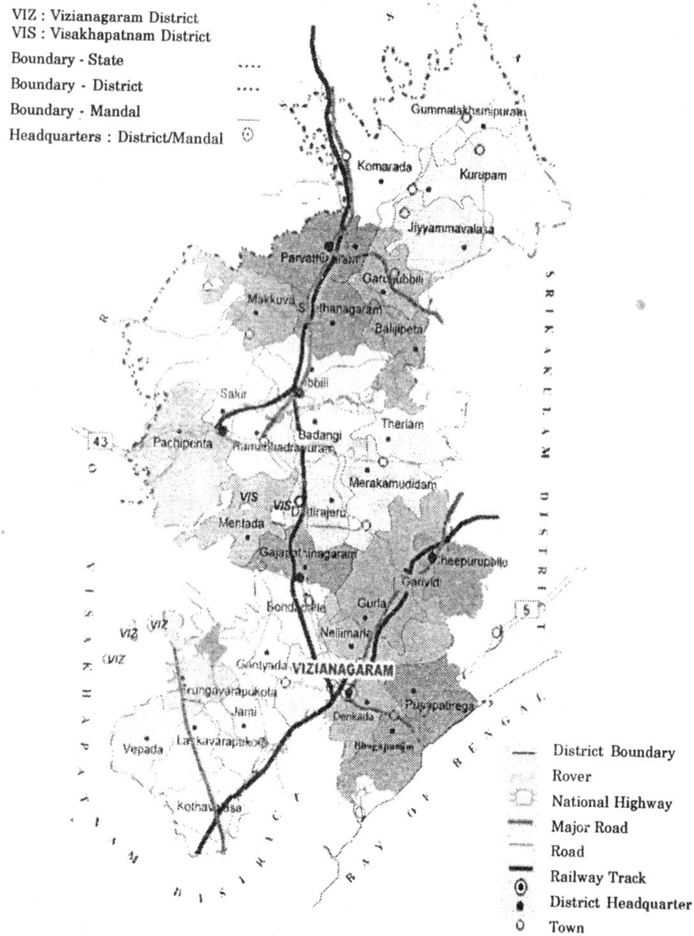

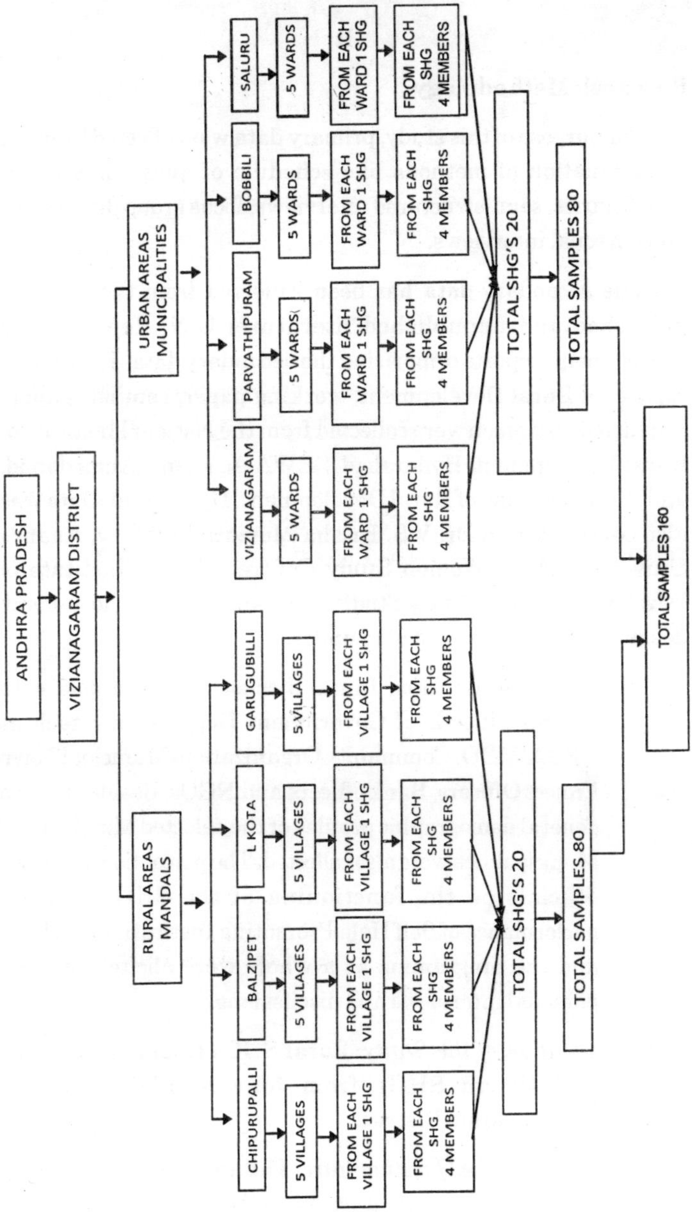
ANDHRA PRADESH
VIZIANAGARAM DISTRICT
URBAN AREAS MUNICIPALITIES
RURAL AREAS MANDALS
VIZIANAGARAM
PARVATHIPURAM
BOBBILI
SALURU
5 WARDS
FROM EACH WARD 1 SHG
FROM EACH SHG 4 MEMBERS
TOTAL SHG'S 20
TOTAL SAMPLES 80
CHIPURUPALLI
BALZIPET
L KOTA
GARUGUBILLI
5 VILLAGES
FROM EACH VILLAGE 1 SHG
FROM EACH SHG 4 MEMBERS
TOTAL SHG'S 20
TOTAL SAMPLES 80
TOTAL SAMPLES 160

II

Research Methodology

For purpose of this study, primary data was collected by using a combination of methods like schedule of questionnaire for beneficiaries; semi-structured interviews, focus group discussions and personal interviews.

The secondary data has been collected from the study of published and unpublished literature: U.N. Reports, and Government Reports comprising the secondary data. The annual reports of Rural Development, working paper, seminar papers conducted on women were collected from the National Institute of Rural Development, Hyderabad, SEWA Academy, Ahmedabad, and State Academy of Rural Development, Hyderabad. Data was also collected from Dr. V.S. Krisha Memorial Library, Andhra University, A.U., Women Study Centre Library, Institute of Development and Planning Studies, Visakhapatnam. The research design adopted is detailed here under.

a) *Primary Discusion:* Initial discussions were held with various officials of Government Departments such as DRDA, MDO, Community Organization, Municipal Town Project Officers, Bank officers and NGOs. Besides these a general demographic profiles of the selected Mandals and Municipalities were also collected. The perception of various officials on the functioning of the SHGs and the performance of Self Help Promoting Institutions (SHPIs) and the programme as a whole were elicited through personal interviews and discussions.

b) *Location of the Study:* Rural SHGs from four Mandals and Urban SHGs from four Municipalities in Vizianagaram District.

c) *Design of the Questionnaire:* The approach to the design of the questionnaire is based on the following criteria.

1. Impressions gathered / observations made during the preliminary visit in the district.
2. Discussions held with the staff.
3. Respondents' ability to comprehend and communicate.

The schedule of questions which was meant for the beneficiaries included the questions regarding their socio-economic background, implementation of the programme; suggestions if any, which the beneficiaries wanted to make. It is a comprehensive and quite an exhaustive schedule that includes thrift and credit, profitability of enterprises, social development and social capital, group dynamics. Levels of empowerment of members were enlisted using multiple parameters, similarly, schedule of questions meant for APOS, TPOS consisted of questions on implementation, monitoring and performance of the programme, role of Mandal Samakya offices. Cluster coordination, attitudes of the various coordinating agencies, administrative problems regarding the functioning of the SHGs, etc. and suggestions if any are also taken into account.

The sample consists of 40 SHGs in Vianagaram district A.P. and to select rural and urban Self Help Groups stratified proportional random sample technique was adopted. In Vizianagaram district to study rural SHGs four Mandals were selected and to study urban SHGs four Municipalities were selected on the basis of performance of SHGs (i.e. developed, under developed and developing SHGs). Thus in each Mandal five SHGs were selected from five villages and from each Municipality five SHGs were selected from five wards for conducting group interviews. From each SHG four group members were selected for in-depth analysis of the study care was taken to cover all caste groups such as SC, ST, Non SC/ST/(OBC/OC).

Table 2.7
Study area sample

S. No.	*State*	*District*	*Mandals*	*Munici-palities*	*No. of SHGs*		*No. of SHG Members*	
					Rural	*Urban*	*R*	*U*
1	A.P.	Vizia-nagaram	Cheepu-rupalli	Viziana-garam	5	5	20	20
2			Balzipeta	Parvathipurm	5	5	20	20
3			L. Kota	Bobbili	5	5	20	20
4			Garugubilli	Saluru	5	5	20	20

Total eighty members from rural SHGs and eighty members from urban SHGs were taken as sample to study. Apart from the SHG members, officials from DRDA, Municipalities, NGOs, women and child development, Bank officers like Lead Bank Manager, Commercial Bank Manager. NABARD were also contacted to elicit their perceptions about the functioning of the SHGs promoted by different functioning agencies.

Field Work

The field work comprised of the following components.

- Interviewing the sample of twenty rural and twenty urban SHGs using the questionnaire.
- Interviews with the Assistant Project Director, Mandal Samakhya Officers, Municipal Town Project Officers with the help of the designed questionnaire.
- Discussion with the officials, NGOs, Bank Managers involved in this programme in Vizianagaram District.

Scope of the study

The present study examines the plight of rural and urban

women, their performance and participation (SHGs), group dynamism and cohesiveness. It is an empirical study and provided an opportunity to bring awareness among women by addressing them on the advantages they gain through working as a group. This programme facilitated capacity building, social mobilization, self-confidence and convergence of services. The research helps in bridging the gap between urban and rural areas, help women to strengthen their economic activities, improve forward-backward linkages and credit needs. The outcomes of the study will definitely identify the lacunae's gives good suggestions to overcome the hurdles faced by SHGs in their functioning and to formulate better policies for their implementation.

Limitation

- This is a process study, not impact study;
- Some of the fields in interview schedule have not been filled in some cases, there is a lot of inconsistency in the collected data and hence the data collected would only be an approximation of actual facts.
- Data pertaining to the number of SHGs formed and functional affectively are not compiled properly and mismatches are noticed.

Tools used

The following are the tools used.

- Interview and schedule
- Personal interview
- Observation and Official documents.

Data Analysis

Since most of the data was qualitative in nature, content analysis was done for drawing inferences.

Hypothesis

It is hypothesized that micro-credit helps to enhance the

resource base of women and micro-finance make women to assert their right to resources. The women participate as subjects and not as objects of development. Community initiatives in the implementation of such measure could therefore make a significant difference and can develop a higher vision about their future in terms of employment generation, marketing chains and access to credit. Thus the present study provides insights into women development and empowerment perspectives.

3

Microfinance and Self Help Group Movement in Andhra Pradesh

An understanding of India's poverty, economy and growth helps in making an informed statement about the importance and impact of Microfinance in India.

Globalization and economic liberalization have opened up tremendous opportunities for development and growth resulting in the modifications of livelihood strategies. However, these changes are making the marginalized and poor sections of society more vulnerable in the absence of adequate safety net. Keeping in view the wide spread poverty, there is need not only to ameliorate the economic conditions of the marginalized and disadvantaged women, but also to transform their social structure. In the context of women, their economic condition becomes more vulnerable due to unequal distribution of resources. Poverty and deprivation increase gender inequality, which favours a policy for empowerment of women by increasing their access to credit though SHGs so as to enable them to acquire the capacity and assets that can help, facilitate and realize strategic gender needs (Sadhan 2004).

The strength of Microfinance sector in India has been significant over last two decades. There exist different approaches and modes of Microfinance; the most predominant in operation among these is SHG model.

It focuses on promoting communication among various stakeholders and incorporates more issues and prospects. Through microfinance, more financial resources are being made available to the bottom of the pyramid; it improves the livelihoods, entrepreneurial skills and finally results in empowerment.

Millions are unable to enjoy their social, political and economic rights partly because they live in extreme poverty. Access to credit and other financial sources could reduce poverty and enable women to effectively realise many other results. Mohammad Yunus founder of the Grameena Bank argued that credit should be recognized as a fundamental human right. In our increasingly capitalistic world, access to micro credit is the ticket, the poor women need to stay afloat and create new possibilities. To have a truly inclusive economy, the world's poorest women need initiatives that jump start their economic activities must not be left out.

It is obvious that making women more productive more effective income earners will reduce their dependency and enhance their status. (A World Bank Country Study: Gender and Poverty in India, The World Bank, Washington D.C.,1991). It will also

1) reduce fertility and slow population growth;
2) improve child survival;
3) increase the share of family income allocated to food and healthcare of children;
4) raise household incomes, especially in families below the poverty line, and
5) increase aggregate labour productivity and speedup growth in key economic factor.

Hence economic success for women will improve their own lives and those of all in accordance with the changing needs of time. Anti-poverty programme have been renamed and restructured to make them more effective and people oriented. One such example is merging self-employment programmes like IRDP, TRYSEM, DWCRA in to one single unit Indira Kranthi Padham. It is quite apparent that the Government is committed to make these programmes more focused and more holistic, aiming to create sustainable assets for long term benefits to the poor women.

Women face a wide range of biases in society against the unequal opportunities in education, employment and asset ownership. The persisting poverty among women is linked to their unequal situations in the labour market, unfair treatment meted out to them under social welfare systems and their subordinate status as well as lack of power in family. Despite considerable progress achieved in recent decades in developing capabilities, their participation in economic and political decision-making remain limited. Credit institutions that require traditional forms of collateral security excludes women as barrower. Different procedures for starting a business, non-availability of credit and lack of political contact prevent women answering an entrepreneurial role.

In short, access to credit resources and gender inequalities undermine women's development. So, improving income generation activities of women through Micro-credit has to be a part of any sustainable strategy for a development (Sen, 1999) (Christa Bell, P.J, p. 29). Raising household incomes can lead to more equal human development for males and females. The expansion of economic opportunities reduces gender disparities. It depends on the availability of income generating activities and their organization (World Bank 2001 b). It is widely accepted that economic participation of poor women is the solution for many problems they face. Economic participation of women is both a reward on its own and a major influence for social change in general. Hence, in the short term women's earnings have a positive effect on incidence and severity of poverty at the household level. In the long term there are important inter-generational effects on the quality of human capital (Bennet, 1992).

From the above observations, it is clear that "the relative respect and regard for women's well-being is strongly influenced by women's ability to earn an independent income, to find employment outside the home, to have ownership rights and to have literacy and be educated participants in decision-making within and outside the family." (Sen, 1999; p.191).

Experience shows that most of the poor women invest wisely and make sound decisions to maximize returns. Access to savings and credit facility helps poor women to make comparatively larger investment and allows them to take the advantage of profitable business opportunities and increase their earning potential. At this juncture to provide small loans and savings facilities to the poor women through a strategy called Microfinance / Micro credit for reducing poverty in all forms was designed by agencies. Micro credit has been defined as "Programs that provide credit for self-unemployment and other financial and business services (including savings and technical assistance) to very poor persons (Micro Credit Summit, 1997)." Nowadays, microfinance represents something more than micro credit – it also refers to savings, insurances, payments and remittances, in sum to a much wider range of financial services (Tankha, 1999). Thus, Microfinance refers to the entire range of financial and non-financial services, including skill upgradation and entrepreneurship development. Micro-finance focuses on women's empowerment and offers a path way out of extreme poverty and towards dignity and security for women, their families and whole communities.

Thus the basic idea of micro-finance is that poor are ready and willing to pull them out of poverty if given access to economic inputs. It not only provides poor women with opportunities for self reliance through entrepreneurship, but also cushions the poor against economic shocks and provides a means of social mobilization in their communities. Investing in women is good business. Given proper access to credit, women mobilize and save, and build assets and their small businesses (Asian Development Bank, 1999).

Vice President Peter Sullivan stressed that investing in poor women is one of the most effective strategies for reducing poverty and improving the status of women. Poor women are bankable as they are good barrowers and good repayers. "Experience has shown that if you give a loan, she will not only repay the loan but will invest the money wisely. Earnings from the investment will feed, clothe, educate and buy medicine for her children. In short, there are multiplier effects of lending to women. Lending to women can empower them. Accessing loans, earning an income, and making a financial contribution to the survival of the family increase a woman's decision-making power with in the household. It gives her a voice where previously she had none.

Through micro finance, women have noted positive change in the way they are treated by the members of their family and their community. According to Women's World Banking (WWB) "Economic empowerment goes hand in hand with increased respect and greater sense of self worth". Microfinance is indeed crucial in helping women make the transition out of poverty.

The typical microfinance clients are low income persons that do not have access to formal financial institutions. Their 'micro-enterprises' represent an estimated 80 percent of urban enterprises and 20 percent of the GNP of their countries. Microfinance clients are typically self-employed, often household-based entrepreneurs. In rural areas, they are usually engaged in agricultural and small income generating activities such as food processing and petty trades. In urban areas, micro finance activities are more diverse and include shopkeepers, service providers, artisans, street vendors etc. Micro finance clients are poor and vulnerable than non-poor who have a relatively stable source of income.

Microfinance brings the power of credit to the grassroots by way of loans to the poor women, without requirement of collateral or previous credit record. Experience shows that microfinance can help the poor to increase income, build viable businesses, and reduce their vulnerability to external shocks. It can also be a powerful instrument for self-empowerment, by enabling the poor women, to become economic agents of change.

A considerable body of literature has accumulated over the past years documenting and monitoring the development of micro-finance sector (Sidney et al. 1997, Fisher and Sriram 2002, Little-field and Rosenberg 2004, T Sai 2004, Dasgupta 2005).

The initial micro credit innovations in disparate settings of Bangladesh, Indonesia and Bolivia demonstrated the success of micro lending to poor without collateral requirements. (Grameen in Bangladesh, Bank Rakayat Indonesia and PRODEM in Bolivia).

Rhyne (2001) observes that these interventions demonstrated techniques for lending to the poor with better out reach and cost recovery. Despite the contextual differences, the unifying thread of these early innovations lay in their certain common principles like reliance on character or peer pressure rather than collateral as loan security, leveraging social capital, positive incentives for repayment and interest rates that approached or covered cost. These innovations acted as catalysts for replication across the globe and their underlying principles continue to form the bedrock of microfinance interventions till date.

The universal appeal of microfinance stemmed from its ability to reach the poor without social collateral and generation of near full recovery rates through what has been described as a win-win proposition. The main streaming of micro finance world wide and its global acceptance in development community is based on this win-win proposition. The progress report submitted by Micro Credit Summit Campaign indicates that as of Dec. 31, 2004, three thousand one hundred and sixty four micro credit institutions have reached 92.27 million clients translating into micro credit interventions having reached 333 million poor families world wide. The obsession with microfinance in development sector is succinctly captured by Remenyi (2000, p 30), "every bilateral donor and NGO seems to believe that it too must be involved in micro finance if it is to retain credibility as a development agency with an option for the poor."

It is claimed that this new paradigm of unsecured small scale financial service provision helps poor women take advantage of economic opportunities, expand their income, smoothen their consumption requirement, reduce vulnerability and also empowers them [CGAP, 2003; ADB 2004].

Former World Bank President James Wolfenshon said "Microfinance fits squarely in to the Bank's overall strategy." The Banks mission is to reduce poverty and improve living standards by promoting sustainable growth and investment in people through loans, technical assistance, and policy guidance. Microfinance contributes directly to this objective. The emphasis on microfinance is reflecting in microfinance being a key feature in Poverty Reduction Strategy Papers (PRSPs).

Realising the importance of microfinance, World Bank has also taken major steps in developing the sector. Formation of Consultative Group to Assist the Poor (CGAP) in 1995 as a consortium of 33 pubic and private development agencies and establishment of Micro finance Management Institution (MFMI) in 2003 are significant landmarks. CGAP acts as a "resource center for the entire microfinance industry where it incubates and supports new ideas, innovative products, cutting-edge technology, novel mechanisms for delivering financial services, and concrete solutions to the challenges of expanding microfinance.

The current literature on microfinance is also dominated by the positive linkages between microfinance and achievement of Millennium Development Goals (MDGs). ADB in its theme chapter on microfinance also cites access to financial services as critical for eliminating poverty and reaching MDGs. In the Indian context, increasing access to credit for the poor has always remained at the core of Indian Planning in fight against poverty.

It was realised that the poor tended to come together in a variety of informal ways for pooling their savings and dispensing small and unsecured loans at varying costs to group members on the basis of the need.

The post-nationalization period in the banking sector, Circa 1969, witnessed a substantial amount of resources being earmarked towards meeting the credit needs of the poor. There were several objectives for the bank nationalization strategy including expanding the outreach of financial services to neglected sectors (Singh, 2005). As a result of this strategy, the banking network underwent an expansion phase without comparables in the world. Credit came to be recognized as a remedy for many of the ills of the poverty. There spawned several pro-poor financial services with the support by both the state and central governments, which included credit packages and programmes customized to the perceived needs of the poor.

While the objectives were laudable and substantial progress was achieved, credit flow to the poor and especially for the poor women remained low. This led to initiatives that were institution driven that attempted to converge the existing strengths of rural banking infrastructure and leverage this to better serve the poor. The pioneering efforts towards this were made by National Bank for Agriculture and Rural Development (NABARD), which was given the tasks of framing appropriate policy for rural credit provision of technical assistance backed liquidity support to banks, supervising rural credit institutions and other development initiatives.

In the early 1980s, Govt. of India launched the Integrated Rural Development Programme (IRDP), a large poverty alleviation credit programme, which provided government subsidized credit through banks to the poor. It was aimed that the poor would be able to use the inexpensive credit to finance themselves over the poverty line.

Also during this period, NABARD conducted a series of research studies independently and in association with Mysore Resettlement and Development Agency (MYRADA), a leading Non Governmental

Organization (NGO) from Southern India, which showed that despite having a wide network of rural bank branches serving the rural poor, a very large number of the poorest of the poor continued to remain outside the fold of the formal banking system. These studies also showed that the existing banking policies, systems and procedures, and deposit and loan products were perhaps not well suited to meet the most immediate needs of the poor. It also appeared that what the poor really needed was better access to these services and products rather than cheap subsidized credit. Against this background, a need was felt for alternative policies, systems and procedures, savings and loan products, other complementary services, and new delivery mechanisms, which would fulfill the requirements of the poorest, especially of the women members of such households. The emphasis therefore was on improving the access of the poor to microfinance rather than just micro credit.

Microfinance is a provision of thrift credit and other financial services and providing very small amounts to the poor in rural, semi-urban or urban areas for enabling them to raise their income levels and improve their living standards (NABARD). To answer the need for microfinance for the poor, the past 25 years has seen a variety of programmes promoted by the government and NGOs. These programmes vary from regional rural banks with a social mandate to Micro Finance Institutions (MFIs). In 1999, the Government of India merged various credit programmes together, refined them and launched a new programme called Swarnajayanthi Gram Swarojgar Yojana (SGSY). The mandate of SGSY is to continue to provide subsidized credit to the poor through banking sector to generate self-employment through a self-help group approach and the programme has grown to an enormous size. In A.P. State the activities of development of women and children in rural areas DWCRA and VELUGU and other self help group programmes were integrated in 2005 under a programme called Indira Kranti Padham. The basic objectives of this integration is to implement various programmes for strengthening of SHGs with similar implementation strategy. This new scheme was designed by clubbing women empowerment with poverty alleviation. It is a statewide poverty reduction project to enable the rural poor to improve their livelihoods and quality of life through their own organization. It aims to cover all the rural poor households in the state. In the rural areas it is implemented by Society for Elimination of Rural Poverty (SERP) and in urban areas by Mission for Elimination of Poverty in Municipal Areas (MEPMA). It focuses on deepening the process, providing an institutional structure and developing a frame work, sustaining it for comprehensive poverty eradication. It is the single largest poverty reduction project in South Asia. The design of the programme is built on combining the "collective wisdom of the poor women, the organizational capabilities of the social intermediary and the financial strength of the Banks".

Table 3.1
Progress of SHG Bank–Linkage in India

Year	*No. of SHGs Linked*
1992-93	255
1997-98	14315
2000-01	263825
2001-02	461478
2002-03	717360
2003-04	1079091
2004-05	1618456
2005-06	2238565
2006-07	2924973

Source: NABARD Annual Reports and SHG Bank linkage data of different years.

The performance highlights of SHG-Bank Linkage programme in India as on March 2008 (during 2007-08) reveals that, banks have financed more than 12.28 lakh SHGs (cumulatively), of which 90 percent are women groups. These SHGs have disbursed loans of more than Rs.8849.41 crores as bank loan against 11,05,749 SHGs with bank loan of Rs.6,570.39 crore during 2006-07 with a growth rate of 11.03 over last FY2006-07. As many as 35,294 bank branches were involved in financing SHGs spread over 563 districts across the country. The progress of the self help movement in India so far has been promising. It has reached out nearly 40.95 million households over the last decade. It has shown that the poor can organize themselves and do things to promote their well being.

In Andhra Pradesh, Self Help Movement through savings has been taken up as mass movement by women. There are about 9 lakh women SHGs in Andhra Pradesh covering nearly 111.81 lakh rural poor women. The SHGs are not only resorting but are also taking small loans out of the corpus available with the group. An amount of Rs.4025.55 crores is mobilized as corpus among these groups and the savings of these SHGs have an accumulated savings Rs.1962.50 as on March, 2009. The state government has taken several initiatives to extend financial support to these groups. During the financial year 2008-09 Rs.11037 crores has been targeted as loan mobilization under SHG-Bank linkage programme and an amount of Rs.7203.53 crores has been mobilized up to March 2009. In Andhra Pradesh more than 52% of SHGs were financed by banks under SHG linkage. This number is more than the all India figure excluding that of Andhra Pradesh. 310488 SHGs were provided repeat finance by banks during 2008-2009 which comes to 76% of total SHGs in the state of Andhra Pradesh. As per the report of the bankers, the recovery of loan is around 95% as against 87% when comparative to other states (www.serp.ap.gov.in/bl).

Table 3.2
Growth of SHGs in AP and Bank Linkages

Year	*Cumulative No. of SHGs linked*	*Cumulative Loan distributed (Rs. in million)*
1999-00	35821	809.82
2000-01	84939	1675.84
2001-02	243714	5212.57
2002-03	281338	9753.87
2003-04	385576	17283.79
2004-05	492927	27460.93

Source: NABARD

Microfinance has evolved over the past quarter century across India in to various operating forms and to a varying degree of success. One such form of microfinance has been the developments of self help movement.

In India self help groups represent a unique approach to financial intermediation. The approach combines access to low-cost financial services with a process of self-management and development for the women who are SHG members. SHGs are formed and supported usually by NGOs or by Government agencies. Linked not only to banks but also to widen developmental programmes, SHGs are seen to confer many benefits, both economic and social. SHGs enable women to grow their savings and to access the credit which banks are increasingly willing to lend.

While no definitive date has been determined for the actual conception and propagation of SHGs, the practice of small groups of rural and urban people bonding together to form a savings and credit organization is well established in India. In the early stages, NGOs played a pivotal role in innovating the SHG model and implementing the model to develop the process fully. In the 1980's, policy-makers took notice and worked with development organizations and bankers to discuss the possibility of promoting these savings and credit groups. Their efforts and the simplicity of SHGs helped to spread the movement across the country. State Government established revolving loan funds which were used to fund SHGs.

Organizations based on the Gandhian philosophy of self-reliance had already been popularized during the freedom movement in British India. In the past years SHGs have been formed as a part of development strategy with a primary focus on poverty alleviation and empowerment of women. It has taken up the concept of self help, as the agenda and to some extent the social base became broader and even more ambitious than the industrialized countries.

Self help is any voluntary action undertaken by an individual or group of individuals who aim at the satisfaction of individual or collective needs or aspirations. The distinctive feature of a self-help initiative or activity is the substantial contribution made from the individual's / group's own sources in terms of labour, capital, land and / or entrepreneurial skills (Subrahmanyam, P.V.V., 2006).

The biggest challenge to any civilized society is the economic deprivation. The most potential tool against deprivation is building human capital among the deprived, through sustainable development initiative which is taken up by the deprived themselves.

Self realization and self-initiative are the two most powerful weapons to wash out poverty from the world map." This dynamic quotation of world's greatest economist Chanakya is been translated to one word that is SHG (Self Help Group). Microfinance through SHG has become a ladder for the poor to bring them up not only economically but also socially, mentally and attitudinally.

SHG is a method of organizing the poor people and marginalized to come together to solve their individual problems. Take the example of the Grameena Bank of Bangladesh, it is the people bank formed by the poor to provide easy loans for themselves. The poor collect their savings and save it in their own banks. In return they receive easy access to loans with a small rate of interest to start their micro credit enterprise. Thousands of the poor and the marginalized population in Bangladesh have built their lives, their families and their society through self help groups. The 9th Five Year Plan of Government of India had given due recognition to the importance and relevance of the SHG method to implement developmental groups at the grassroot level.

What is self help?

Self help is a trust belief and conviction that the community, no matter how backward, has resources that can be mobilized for meeting individual's local needs and that of the community for making local improvement and bring about social change.

Villages, semi-urban and urban areas are faced with problems related to poverty, illiteracy, lack of skills, health care etc. These are problems that cannot be tackled individually but can be better answered through group efforts. Today these groups known as SHGs have become the vehicle of change for the poor and marginalized.

What are SHGs?

- SHG is a development group for the poor and marginalized.
- It is recognized by the government and does not require any formal registration.
- The purpose of the SHG is to build functional capacity of the poor and the marginalized in the field of employment and income generating activities.
- People are responsible for their own future by organizing themselves into SHGs.

Guiding principles for formation of SHG

The strong belief by the individual to bring about change through collective efforts.

- Effort to build on mutual trust and mutual support.
- Every individual is equal and responsible.
- Every individual is committed to the cause of the group.
- The belief and commitment by the individual that through the group their standard of living will improve.
- Savings are the foundation on which the group is built for collective action.

It is imperative that SHG should be promoted in the way that facilities a co-operative participative and empowerment culture. (Ritu Jain et al., 2007).

The Self Help Groups provide economic benefits in certain areas of production process by undertaking common action programmes, like cost-effective credit delivery system, generating a forum for collective; learning with rural people promoting democratic culture fostering on entrepreneurial culture, providing a firm base for dialogue and co-operation in programmes with other institutions, processing creditability and power to ensure participation and helping to access an individual members management capacity. (Fernandez, 1995).

Features of SHGs and Linkage programme

Decision-making	Members make decisions collectively. SHG concept offers opportunities for participative decision-making on conduct of meetings thrift and credit decisions. The participative process makes the group a responsible barrower.
Financial services	SHGs provide the needed financial services to the members at their doorstep. The rural poor needs different types of financial

	services, viz. Savings, consumption credit, production credit, insurance, remittance facilities etc. The platform of SHGs provides the possibility to converge these services.
Supplementary for formal banking	SHG linkage does not supplement the existing banking system, but it supplements it thus taking full advantage of the resources and other advantages of the banking system.
Cutting costs	SHG linkage cuts costs for both banks and borrowers. In a study sponsored by FDC, Australia. It was observed that the reduction in costs for the bankers is around 40% as compared to IRDP loans. The poor have a net advantage of 85% as compared to individual borrowing. Similar finding was also observed in a NABARD study.
NPA Survey	The linkage mechanism has proved that the repayments are a higher 95% - 100%.
Peer pressure as collateral	The SHG linkage emphasizes peer pressure within the group as collateral substitute.
Quality clients	The SHGs are turning to be quality clients in view of better credit management, mobilization of thrift, low transaction costs and near full repayments.
Clients preparation	The members of the SHGs could over a period of time, very selectively graduate to the stage of micro entrepreneurship and have been prepared with requisite credit discipline.
Social agenda	Available statistics indicate dependency of 35% to 40% rural households on non-institutional sources for credit needs. SHG linkage offers a better way of dealing with the magnitude of social agenda. Many NGOs/ Governments have recognized the SHG as a vehicle for carrying and depending of their developmental agenda/ delivery service.
Exclusive poor focus	SHGs have exclusive focus on absolute have nots, who have been by passed by the

	banking system. Social banking does not have any meaning if the lowest strata and unreached are not focused.
No subsidy dependence syndrome	The programme does not envisage any subsidy support from the government in the matter of credit. The issue is to build capabilities and enterprise of the individual members, blending with group cohesion and solidarity through training provided by a SHPI to set the ball rolling for the SHG.

[*Source:* Kropp, E.W. and Suran, B.S. 2002; Linkage Banks and Self Help Groups in India – An Assessment]

A.P's vision on SHG movement

Each family in the state should be out of poverty and enjoy :

- Life with dignity.
- Equity within the family.
- Freedom from hunger.
- Decent income of more than Rs.5,000 per month through 3 or 4 sources.
- Planned household expenditure.
- Risk management – life, health, assets and incomes.
- Shelter, sanitation, drinking water, good health and
- Education.

Presently, under the rural programme facilitated by the Society for the Elimination of Rural Poverty (SERP), an independent organization of A.P government, there are about 7,08,395 rural SHGs which receive support and monitoring from 34,269 village organizations. These village organizations in turn are supported by 1086 Mandal Samakyas. In response to the remarkable success of SHG model in reducing rural poverty, more than 1,75,000 SHGs have been established in 124 municipal towns and 1574 slum level federations have been credited within 68 municipal towns.

The Conceptual Framework: SHGs in Andhra Pradesh

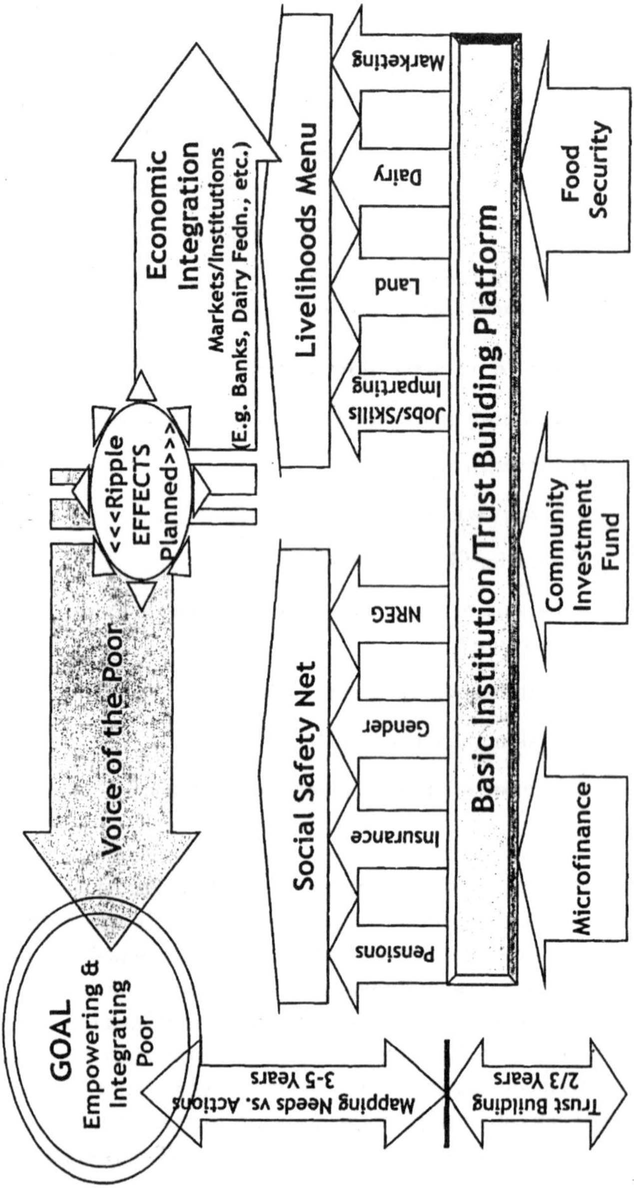

Presently, the urban programme is in the process of being extended to all municipalities under the 'Mission for Elimination of Poverty in Municipal Areas' (MEPMA) an organization that has been promoted and are functioning in the urban area.

In Vizianagaram district under SHG programme, as on March 2010, there are 29,888 SHGs in rural areas and in urban areas 5,282 SHGs are functioning. The profile of the rural and urban SHGs and their performance is elaborated in the next chapter.

4

Profile and Performance of SHGs: Rural Vs Urban

In the previous chapter a reference was made about the poverty of women and how micro-finance is making a headway in its efforts to reduce poverty and empower the poor women. Now, the profile and performance of SHGs – rural and urban will be discussed. SHGs were formed in the rural and urban areas with the assumption that they will come together for mutual assistance in satisfying a common need, overcoming a common handicap or life disrupting problems and bring about a desired social and personal change. SHGs emphasize face-to-face interactions with emphasis- on personal responsibility by the numbers.

There is a high demand for micro-finance and it is not limited to rural society or developing countries only. It is equally applicable to urban society and developed countries as well. Development alone cannot bring peace and prosperity unless social justice and gender equality are ensured. It is well recognized that various developmental programmes have bypassed women who constitute about half of the population of the country. International conventions, conferences, legal enactments and constitutional provisions at the national level highlighted the need for gender equality and women empowerment.

The SHGs became a regular component of Indian financial system since 1996. The SHGs are small, informal and homogeneous groups. These groups have proved themselves as cyclic agents of development in both rural and urban areas. One of the powerful approaches to women empowerment and entrepreneurship is the formation of SHGs among women. SHGs are necessary to overcome exploitation, create confidence for the economic self-reliance of the women in poverty who are mostly invisible in the social structure.

Microfinance as a tool of poverty alleviation has gained acceptance in development dialogue all over the world. There is acute need among the poor for credit, both for consumption and production, which often form the declining line between survival and succumbing to poverty. Thus poverty reduction is the envisioned objective of micro-finance. Development experience shows gender inequalities are a major factor impeding progress towards Millennium Development Goals of poverty reduction. Further, these gender disparities are acute among rural and urban counterparts. As a result of disparities and imbalances between rural and urban women, there is a disparity in women empowerment also.

"Real India exists in villages" said the Father of the Nation Mahatma Gandhi. However despite all the efforts even after six decades of Independence one of the aspects of the country is the vast difference in terms of poverty and facilities in rural and urban areas.

A brief account of rural and urban dichotomy with particular reference to women and the disparities existing in the study area was examined in the previous chapter. In India the urban population has increased by more than 1000 percent between 1901 and 2001, fueled largely by migration from the rural areas, the place of origin to urban locations, mainly because of increase of employment and better resources.

While India has a long tradition of urbanization which has continued since the days of Indus Valley Civilization, the current spate of migration from rural to urban locations has been driven by poverty, unemployment, natural calamities and under-development at the original places. This chapter examines the profile of the rural and urban women self help group members which is mainly a comparative study, backed by field studies. Further it will also evaluate how IKP for rural and urban women provide better income and employment opportunities to large group of landless, unskilled, illiterate labourers in these areas. This program is meant not only for the balanced regional development but also to reduce unacceptable disparities between rural and urban women. This program helps women and their family to increase their income, learns new skills, improve their social status, built-up assets and improve their quality of life. It is also one of the felt needs to consider the way in which development policies are implemented and the impact of these policies on household livelihood strategies. Again in this era of globalization, agriculture itself is not providing a reliable resource of income to rural women. High cost of cultivation, scarcity of irrigation water, stagnation of productivity in this sector and fluctuations in the prices of agriculture products are some of the factors responsible for converting agriculture in to a non-profitable sector of employment. In such 'distress' condition, this IKP program is a boon for the women in poverty, which provides them employment and income generation for better livelihood. This study focuses both on rural and urban SHGs and considers them not as competitive but treats them as complementary to each other because rural and urban areas constitute parts of an organic whole, which paves the way for balanced development and poverty alleviation.

It is expected that a scheme like IKP, wherein all related schemes for rural and urban women development are being converged for a synchronized delivery of services. In this back-drop this exercise is undertaken to examine the profile of the rural and urban women SHG members. The profile, performance and strategy of the groups are based on many factors that include the composition of the groups, the leadership, style of functioning, member participation, group performance, resource mobilization and management, interaction with other groups etc.

Caste composition

The caste component of the SHG is diverse across the Mandals and Municipalities and it reveals that out of the total sample of 80 members in rural areas about 37.5 percent belong to SC and 12.5 percent belong to ST and BC and OBC constitute 25 percent. This is illustrated in the Table 4.1 and figure 4.1

Table - 4.1
Distribution of respondents according to caste in rural and urban

S. No.	*Caste*	*Rural N = 80*	*Rural %*	*Urban N = 80*	*Urban %*	*Total N=160*	*Total %*
1	SC	30	37.5	10	12.5	40	25.00
2	ST	10	12.5	20	25	30	18.75
3	BC	20	25	40	50	60	37.50
4	OBC	20	25	10	12.5	30	18.75
Total		80		80	100	160	100

It can be observed that BCs (50 percent) are predominant in the urban areas. STs are 25 percent. SCs and OBCs constitute 12.5 percent respectively. On the whole a clear focus on the backward class community is seen in the study area.

Distribution of respondents according to caste in rural and urban

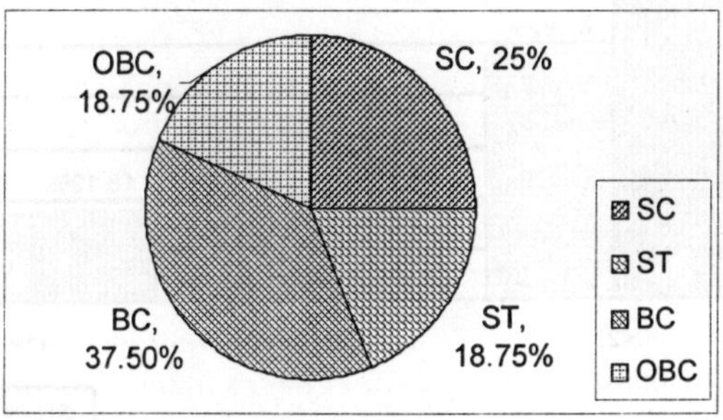

Fig 4.1

Age group of the members

The study reveals that a majority of SHG members in rural areas (58.90%) belong to the age group of 26-40. 18.2 percent belong to the age group below 25 and the rest of the 32.98 percent belongs to the group of age 41 and above. Whereas in urban areas, about 47.82 percent of the members belong to the age group of 26 – 40. 17.28 percent of the members belong to the age group of 25 and below and the rest of the 35.90 percent belongs to the age of 41 and above. This is illustrated in the Table 4.2 and figure 4.2.

Table - 4.2

Distribution of respondents according to their age

S. No.	*Age*	*Percentage in rural area N=80*	*Percentage in urban area N=80*
1.	Below 25	18.2%	17.28%
2.	26 - 40	58.90%	47.82%
3.	41 and above	32.98%	35.90%

Distribution of respondents according to their age

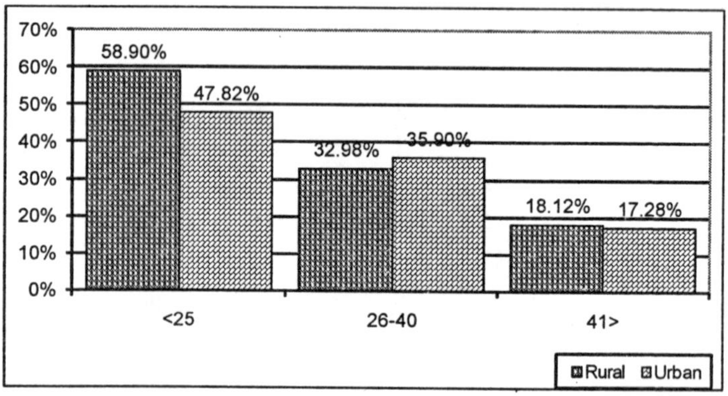

Fig: 4.2

Religion-wise classification

Out of a total sample of 160 SHG members in 4 Mandals and 4 Municipalities of Vizianagaram district, the religion-wise classification is shown below fig. 4.3.

The below figure demonstrates the comparative status of the religion the SHG members - rural Vs urban areas. Over 92.6 percent of total members in the rural area are Hindus whereas 2.52 percent are Muslims and the rest of 4.88 percent are Christians. In urban area, 90.01 percent are Hindus, 3.02 percent are Muslims and 6.97 percent are Christians. The table 4.3 shows the statistical representation of fig 4.3.

Table - 4.3

Distribution of respondents according to their religion

S. No.	*Religion N = 80*	*% in rural area N = 80*	*% in urban area N = 80*
1.	Hindu	92.60%	90.01%
2.	Muslim	02.52%	03.02%
3.	Christian	4.88%	06.97%

Distribution of respondents according to their religion

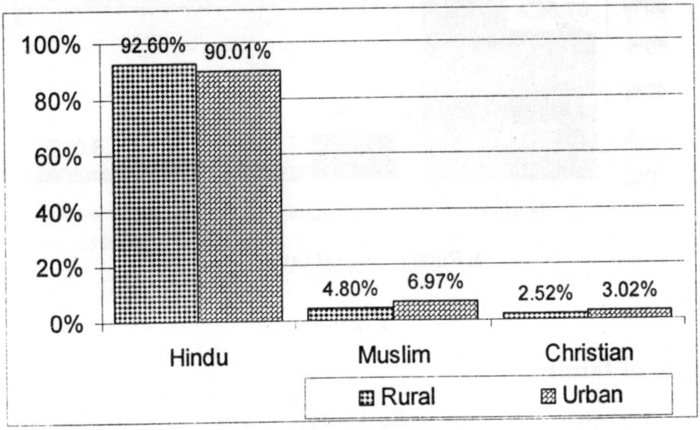

Fig. 4.3

Type of family

The family structure of the beneficiaries is shown below Table 4.4 and fig.4.4. In the rural areas, 67.88 percent adopted nuclear family structure, 10.12 percent are in joint family system and 22 percent are the women headed families. However in urban areas, 86.72 percent preferred nuclear family, 7.28 percent are in joint family system and about 6 percent are the women headed families.

Table 4.4
Distribution of respondents according to their type of family

S. No.	*Family*	*% in rural area N = 80*	*% in urban area N = 80*
1.	Nuclear	67.88%	86.72%
2.	Joint	10.12%	07.28%
3.	Women Headed family	22.00%	06.00%

Distribution of respondents according to their type of family

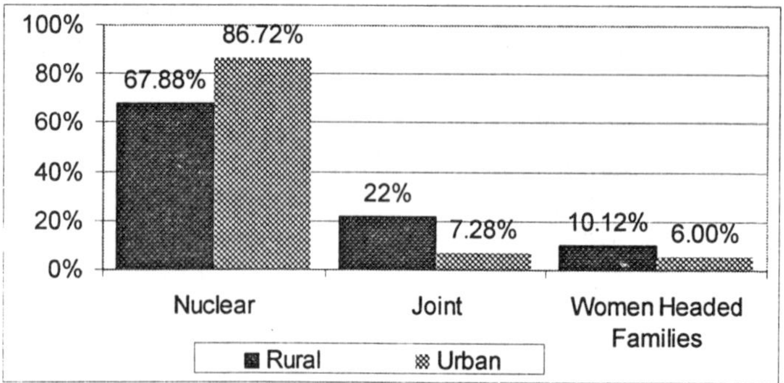

Fig 4.4

Size of family

It is apparent from the fig 4.5, family size of the beneficiaries having 4 people per family is about 91.20 percent and 8.80 percent comes under the family size of 5 and above in case of rural area. In the urban areas, the family of 4 people is about 86.74 percent and 13.26 percent of the beneficiaries come under the family size of 5 and above.

Table 4.5
Distribution of respondents according to their size of family

S. No.	*Size*	*% in rural area N=80*	*% in urban area N=80*
1.	1- 4	91.20%	86.74%
2.	5 and above	08.80%	13.26%

Distribution of respondents according to their size of family

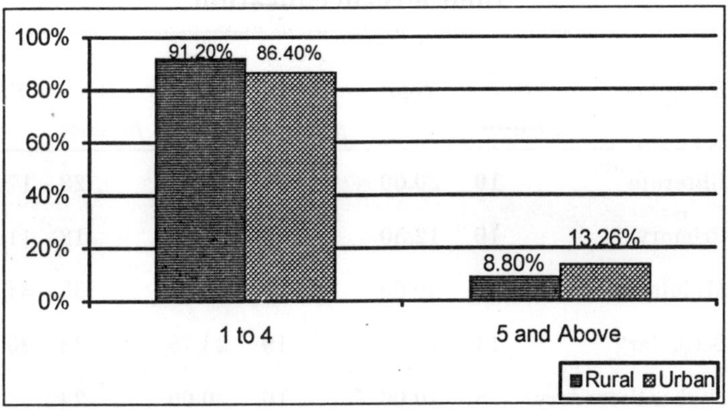

Fig 4.5

Educational status of the members

Among different variables for human development, education is perhaps the most important attribute. Education gives people a sense of independent judgment and power to distinguish between good and bad. Education creates self-discipline and the power to think rationally. It broadens the mind and becomes an instrument of socio-economic change. A minimum level of education is absolutely essential for the active participation of women in the development programme. In fact education is one of the most essential inputs of women empowerment process. It is found that there is a high degree of correlation between the level of education and productivity among the women. Education helps to enhance self esteem and self confidence of women. It builds a positive image of women by recognizing their contribution to the society, polity and economy. It can remove ignorance, superstition and disinclination to accept change. Hence, the data relating to the educational level of respondents is shown in Table 4.6.

Table 4.6
Distribution of respondents according to their level of education

Level of Education	*No. of Bene-ficiaries*	*% of Total*	*No. of Bene-ficiaries*	*% of Total*	*No. of Bene-ficiaries*	*% of Total*
Illiterate	16	20.00	12	15.00	28	17.50
Primary	10	12.50	08	10.00	18	11.25
Middle	32	40.00	23	28.75	55	34.37
Secondary	14	17.25	19	23.75	33	20.62
Higher Secondary	8	10.00	16	20.00	24	15
Graduate	-	-	2	2.50	2	1.25
Total	80	100	80	100	160	100

In the case of rural area out of 80 women, 16 women (20 percent) were totally illiterate. It may be noted 12.50 percent had the ability to read and write, 40 percent studied upto middle school level, 17.2 percent had secondary education. 10 percent had higher secondary education and there is no graduate from the sample of rural areas. Whereas in the case of urban areas illiterates constituted 15 percent, 10 percent of the education upto primary level, 28.75 percent of them were educated upto middle school, followed by secondary 33 percent, higher secondary level 24 percent and constitutes 2.5 percent graduates. If we compare both in rural and urban areas highest number of women comes under the category of middle school level, and they could not take up any other form of employment requiring high skill and formal education. So they were motivated to join the SHGs and start micro-enterprises.

Marital status of the respondents

Distribution of respondents according to the marital status in Rural and urban areas is shown in Table 4.7.

Table 4.7
Distribution of respondents according to their marital status

Marital status	*Rural Areas*		*Urban areas*		*Total*	
	No. of Bene-ficiaries	*% of Total*	*No. of Bene-ficiaries*	*% of Total*	*No. of Bene-ficiaries*	*% of Total*
Married	68	85	70	87.5	138	86.25
Unmarried	08	10	08	10	16	10
Widowed / divorced	04	5	02	2.5	06	3.75
Total	80	100	80	100	160	100

It could be noted that 85 percent of respondents in rural areas and 87.5 percent in urban areas were married. The unmarried constituted 10 percent in both rural and urban areas. Among the rural beneficiaries 5 percent and among the urban SHG members 2.5 percent were widowed.

Table 4.8
Occupational background of the households

Marital Occupation	*Rural Areas*		*Urban areas*		*Total*	
	No. of Beneficiaries	*Percentage of Total*	*No. of Beneficiaries*	*Percentage of Total*	*No. of Beneficiaries*	*Percentage of Total*
Salaried work	2	2.5	6	7.5	8	4.75
Casual labour (including agricultural labour)	52	65	48	60	100	62.5
Petty business	16	20	18	22.5	34	21.25
Artisans	10	12.5	08	10	18	11.25
Total	80	100	80	100	160	100

Majority of the SHG women in both rural and urban areas preferred casual labour as their chief occupation. This is more evident in rural areas 65 percent as compared to urban areas 60 percent. Salaried workers 2.5 percent, artisans 12.5 percent and petty business 20 percent, was the next significant occupation in rural areas. While in urban areas 7.5 percent constituted salaried work, Artisans 10 percent and 22.5 percent were under the category of petty business. This is shown in Table 4.8.

Income levels of the Households

The members were classified in to four categories on the basis of their annual income, before joining the scheme is shown in Table 4.9.

Table 4.9
Income level of households

Range of Income Rs.	*Rural Areas*		*Urban areas*		*Total*	
	No. of Bene-ficiaries	*% of Total*	*No. of Bene-ficiaries*	*% of Total*	*No. of Bene-ficiaries*	*% of Total*
5000-10000	02	2.5	03	3.75	05	3.125
10001-11500	58	72.5	54	67.5	112	70
11501-13600	14	17.5	16	20	30	18.75
13600 and >	06	7.5	07	8.75	13	8.125
Total	80	100	80	100	160	100

It can be seen out of 80 members in the rural areas 6 persons (7.5 percent) had an income of Rs.13600 per annum, 14 persons (17.5 percent) had an income of Rs.11500 but less than Rs.13600. Two members (2.5 percent) were earning between Rs.5000 to 10000 and 58 members (72.5 percent) had an annual income between Rs.10001 to Rs.11500 respectively.

A similar trend could be observed in the case of urban areas also. A majority of the members 67.5 percent were in the category of Rs.10001 to 115001 and 20 percent were members in the category of Rs.11501 to 13600 and 8.75 percent were in the category of Rs.13600 per annum. Only 3.75 percent were under the category of Rs.5000 – 10000 out of 160 samples of respondents, only 8.125 percent belonged to the highest income group of Rs.13600 and above per annum.

Distribution of SHGs across the SHPIs

SHGs across the district are promoted by the Banks and Government institutions. Across 4 Mandals, DRDA is the chief organization promoting the SHGs. SHGs promoted by DRDA are 90 percent and in the urban areas banks play a vital role in promoting SHGs, which is coming to 65 percent. This low participation in urban areas is because the awareness generated in the urban areas is expedited only in 2004 after amalgamation of the SHGs of the rural and urban under one programme by Andhra Pradesh state government.

Age of the SHGs and Federation

A majority of the SHG in the rural areas have been in existence under DWCRA groups since 1987. Now the nomenclature is changed as IKP. It could be noted that 60 percent of the groups formed before 1987 to 2004 and only 40 percent of SHGs were formed during 2004 to 2009. This is the result of the introduction of IKP in AP, and there is promotion of the SHGs all over the district. In the rural areas the movement took a faster pace when compared to urban areas. Total number of groups in Vizianagaram in rural areas as on March 2010 is 29,888 whereas for the urban areas, which include all the 4 municipalities, number of SHG in existence as on March 2010 is only 5282.This reveals in urban SHG have not gained much momentum when compared to rural areas. Accordingly in rural areas, the groups are sustained groups because they were in existence for more than 7 years and in the urban areas the groups have not yet stabilized. Only 12 SHGs were graded and identified as sustained groups.

Performance of the SHGs

Management of thrift and credit

To start with, SHG begins as a thrift group and mobilizes group funds through regular contribution from each member. This group fund is largely utilized by the SHG to provide loans to the members to meet their immediate consumption needs. Prioritization of granting group loans, interest rate repayment pattern etc., are finalized through group consensus. All these transactions are carried out in the group meetings which are conducted regularly as mutually agreed upon by the group members. The group members maintains various books and registers such as attendance register, minutes book, savings ledger, loan ledger, receipt and payment register etc. The group functioning is monitored by the promoting agencies periodically.

The credit management capabilities learnt through group will form the basis for the group cohesiveness and establish group creditability and credit worthiness with the banks.

- It is found that overall monthly savings amount ranged between Rs.30 – 50.

- Monthly savings practice is a most common practice among rural areas 85 percent and in urban areas 82 percent. Around 15 Percent in rural areas and 18 percent in urban areas have adopted weekly savings.

- In the rural areas out of 80 respondents, 54 members (67.5 percent) have taken loans from their corpus at least once over a period of three years. 32.5 percent have not availed a single loan due to inadequate loan amount. Whereas in urban areas out of 80 respondents, 60 members (75 percent) have taken loan from the corpus fund and 25 percent not availed a single loan expecting bigger loans from the banks.

- In the rural areas 74 percent of the beneficiaries and in the urban areas 72 percent of the beneficiaries are aware of the self help group strategy. They also stated that saving money, meeting family expenditure, access to bank credit, getting loans from the bank at low interest rate are some of the objectives of forming self help groups. The study revealed that both in rural and urban areas officials played a dominant role in the formation and promotion of SHG when compared to NGOs.

- Women in the study area expressed various reasons for joining the SHGs. It could be observed that the foremost motivational factor for joining the SHGs in the rural areas seem to be getting credit 47.5 percent, followed by promotion of savings habit 27.5 percent, access to bank 18 percent and to realize socio-economic empowerment 7 percent. Where as in the urban areas the strong motivational factor for joining SHG seems to be for getting credit 58 percent, followed by the promotion of savings habit 22 percent, access to bank 18 percent and to realize socio economic empowerment is 2 percent. So it is evident that both in rural and urban areas the prime motive of the members to join SHG is to obtain micro-credit and for having access towards banks.

Grading of SHGs is taken up periodically to assess the strength and performance of the groups. Grading of groups serves a useful purpose not only for establishing credit linkage with banks but more importantly to understand the strength and effectiveness of the groups. This would help in identifying training needs and plan capacity building programmes.

IKP has given the guidelines for credit linkage of SHGs with banks, which are to be periodically assessed and upgraded. The data from the study indicates, though DRDA identified the rural groups as developed groups, only 85 percent were passed in grade A and 15 percent in grade - B. But overall, the majority of the rural SHG are active groups, whereas in the urban area only 60 percent are grade A and 25 percent stated that their SHGs have not been graded at all and 15 percent of the groups were not aware whether their SHGs have been graded or not.

This is an area of concern because SHGs will be provided with financial assistance only on the basis of their grading. Banks are abnormally delaying gradation and loan process denying even loan to quality groups leading to disillusionment and collapse of SHGs. It is very important to look into the assistance of financial resources because the nurturing of SHGs depends on the financial resources only. This delay is more so in the case of urban SHGs than the rural SHGs.

Sources of funds

The SHGs start with their own savings and internal lending and prove themselves credit worthy. This makes them eligible to access other sources of funding which can be in the form of community investment funds (from DRDA) bank loans and subsidiary for specific marginalized groups from SC or BC corporation.

The activities of the selected SHG groups were basically related to promoting the habit of savings and thrift among the member with income generation activities and asset creation efforts. The savings and lending procedures adopted by group member was very simple and based on trust and confidence. As a democratic body, all the members had the freedom to express their views and decisions were taken unanimously after thorough discussion amongst them. The purpose of loans provided was need based and prioritization among different purposes and members collective decision.

The quantity of money saved by the members ranged from Rs.30 to Rs.50 per head per month. In the rural area, a large magnitude of 90 percent of the groups saved Rs.30 per head per month and the remaining 10 percent of the groups saved Rs.50 per head per month. It has been observed that 99 percent of the groups in the rural areas and 8 percent in the urban areas reached 100 percent level of savings, which is highly appreciable, which reveals that the members in these groups were regular and prompt in contributing their savings and 15 percent of the groups in urban area and 1 percent in rural area were irregular in their savings. Perhaps this is the reason why the bank linkage is poor in the case of urban SHGs relatively.

Sources of Income of thrift contribution made by SHG members in the study area

It was learnt from the members of the rural SHGs that some members borrowed a huge amount of money from the SHGs for various domestic purposes like repairing houses, daughter's marriage etc. While in urban SHGs less number of borrowers utilized the loans for the business purpose such as setting up of pan shops, tailoring and vegetable vending etc

The members generally agreed to divide group loans in rotations on the basis of consumption/business priorities without involving themselves in conflicts where all were in need of loans. The decision-making power rested on the members. The maximum repayment period for the loans was fixed at 12 months. In the extreme cases, if the loan was not repaid in the scheduled months, the least interest due was to be paid for that month. Discussions with the members showed that groups exercise pressure on the defaulters in the form of collecting penalty. The interest rate change did not vary among the groups. Members showed maturity in running organization. Though they were entrusted with the power of fixing their rate of interest, and were aware of using it as a resulting tool and rationalized way to credit, they did not want to cause much inconvenience to their members by hiking interest rates. The SHGs charged a uniform interest rate of 24 percent irrespective of the loan amount. The number of installments for the repayment of the loan was usually fixed by the groups. The repayment of the loan starts with the month following the loan disbursal.

Sources and mobilization of funds

It is quite evident that most of groups across the district let it be rural or urban SHGs, have built group corpus by their regular thrift followed by the funds under IKP. It must be mentioned here that a sizeable amount of bank and to a certain extent government loans under State management was used by SHGs both in urban and rural areas. The average loan amount received by each member from various sources is Rs.14,948 in rural and in urban areas it is Rs.14,244 respectively. This is an amount to generate regular employment and to come out of poverty.

In this study, if we observe the disbursement of funds caste wise BC's seems to be benefiting to a larger extents in accessing the loans from various programmes in urban area and SCs occupy next place followed by OBs and to a much larger extent by STs in rural areas. When it comes to urban areas SC seems to be benefiting to a larger extent in accessing loans from various programs. BC comes next closely followed by STs and to a much lesser extent OCs.

In general on an average IKP groups received more loan amount when compared to non-IKP groups. This could be due to community investment funds available to the groups under IKP.

Overall, rural SHGs have greater cohesiveness, collective decision-making power and better leadership when compared to urban areas as perceived by the functionaries.

In the urban areas most of the groups have not clearly delineated the roles and responsibilities of members and an office bearer in the group. To that extent cohesion is weakening over a period.

The groups studied are 2 – 5 years and it is expected that they would have developed healthy group cohesiveness over these years. However, the study reveals that in municipalities, where groups are less than 3 years old, this process needs continuous nurturing.

In the name of convergence, women were overburdened with responsibilities to take up multiple roles simultaneously in rural areas. Lack of participation by all members in decision-making even after few years in the groups is visible across municipalities.

IKP is different from earlier programmes in terms of the strategy envisaged for its implementation. It has been conceived as a holistic programme, covering all aspects of both rural and urban women. Viz. organizing poor women in to SHGs, capacity building, training, selection of key activities, forming federations, building infrastructure and marketing support.

A major shift of the IKP from the erstwhile programmes is in terms of its emphasis on social mobilization of the poor. A detailed note on social mobilization and income generation activities were discussed in the next chapter.

5

Social Mobilization and Income Generating Activities of Rural and Urban SHGs

The relationship between gender and poverty is a complex and controversial one that is being debated for more than ever before. It is a universally recognized fact that women are poorer than men. Thus in A.P. targeting women has become one more vehicle for gender sensitive poverty alleviation programme. Poor women have become the explicit focus of policy making in the areas of micro credit programmes and income generating activities.

However, the universal validity of the feminization of poverty is being empirically challenged. In this study, poverty is being viewed as a process, rather than as a static concept. For example, the poor women, rather than being viewed as passive victims of society, in need of handouts, are viewed as agents who struggle to cope with poverty with whatever assets they may possess. The emphasis is on the assets they own and resources they can access rather than on what they lack. Along these lines, the related literature has focused on the coping mechanism of the poor. The concept of assets has been extended to include social capital and household relations (Moser 1996, 1998).

Further more, a new qualitative, as opposed to quantitative, approaches to poverty assessment have emphasized the poor woman's own criteria of poverty as well as their own solutions (Chambers 1996). The policy implications of this new approach have emphasized the programme that enable the poor women to exercise their agency, their own solutions and creativity by creating an environment as well as making available critical external resources such as credit. Empowerment of the poor women is viewed as critical to the success of poverty elimination. Poverty eradication is an aspect of human development which is defined as "a process of enlarging people's choices" (UNDP 1990). Development has to be human centric. Development involves change and change involves complex interactions among SHGs in different segments of society, who hold different attitudes, values and interests. Changes made within one group affect other groups. Thus, there is a need to tackle the complex tasks of eliminating poverty through social mobilization and income generating activities.

Social mobilization, as defined by UNICEF is a broad scale movement, engaging people's participation in achieving a specific development goal through self reliant efforts. It involves all relevant segments of the society like SHGs, communities and individuals. It is a planned decentralized process that seeks to facilitate change for development through a range of players engaged in interrelated and complementary efforts. It takes into account the felt needs of the women, embraces the critical principles of community involvement, and seeks to empower women and groups for action. Mobilizing the necessary resources, disseminating information tailored to targeted audiences, generating inter-sectoral support and fostering cross-professional alliances are also part of the process. While the components of the process may be every day practice in many developmental programmes, they tend to be taken up in isolation of each other. But the social mobilization in total aims at a continuum of activities in a broad strategic framework. The process encompasses dialogue and partnership with a wide spectrum of social elements. In short, social mobilization calls for a journey among partners and results in the successful transformation of development goals into societal action.

Social Mobilization Process

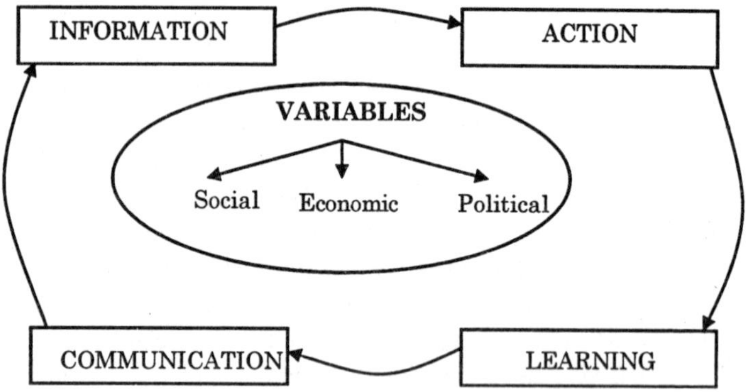

Fig 5.1

Basic Elements / Variables of Social Mobilization:

1. Social	2. Economic	3. Political
Education, health environment	Income generating activities	Decision-making

Social mobilization occupies a central place with a primary focus on working with the poor women. In this particular context, it is a participatory process to raise awareness, mobilize and involve local institutions, local leadership and local communities to organize for collective action towards their common purpose and address collective and individual needs with a primary focus on the poor women. This programme provides social guidance to poor women and facilitates them in harnessing their potential to help themselves. It has organized the poor women in to SHGs to facilitate delivery of services and supplies to them by government and other development agencies and nurtured them in to a self-reliant organization.

Self help and self-reliance is to take a central place in social mobilization as defined by Koenrad Verhegan, (Royal Tropical Institute, The Netherlands 1987). Self help is any voluntary action undertaken by an individual or a group of persons for the satisfaction of individual or group needs. Traditionally, contribution by community in shape of land, money and manpower is known as self-help. But in this program, self-help is seen as women's contribution and the aspirations towards the achievements of self-reliance at the group level. This does not mean that self-help at the individual and household level is not important. But the poor women have no other option without co-operating with each other and pooling of resources to achieve economies of scale. Organizing for collective actions, pooling of resources, formation of equity capital and upgradation of human skills to provide technical and managerial services to its members are the steps of self-help towards achieving self-reliance.

Moreover this programme provides institutional framework for promoting self-help at the community level where they are willing to do something for themselves. Self-help is a mean to achieve self-reliance. Self-reliance is a state of condition whereby a group achieved such condition, where they no longer depend on the assistance of the third party to secure their interest. Self-reliance should not be confused with self-sufficiency.

Further, Human Resource Development and capacity building has very close relationship with social mobilization. Hence, social mobilization is a process of harnessing women's potential through creating awareness, education, training and motivation to become ready for collective actions, which is not possible without proper training. As social mobilization develops, it takes advantage of constantly evolving communication tools and technologies.

Thus this programmes emphasizes on:

- the need to be creative in conducting social mobilization activity by maximizing the use of available communication tools and technology.

- support capacity building.
- support community organization to be sensitive to gender issues and to represent the 'poorest of the poor' and their interests.
- facilitate the creation of local prospects of options for resource generation.

Thus optimism is the gamut of areas in which social mobilization process takes place that can put a greater control in the hands of women in a wide and continuously expanding form in managing water distribution at the village level to standing for local elections and having access to lifelong learning opportunities. (Nath, Vikas 2001). In the context of SHGs, social mobilization has a vital role to play. It is the first and the most crucial step in bringing together and organizing women from identical socio-economic strata into a group. The cohesiveness, identity performance and efficiency of the group to a larger extent depend on the process of social mobilization. This holds good both in homogeneous and heterogeneous groups. Social mobilization has to be a continuous and ongoing process. It has a key role in enabling the poor to realise their own potential, as well as develop linkages and partnerships with the wider society. This would mean taking an active role in the development process as a whole – having access to institutions, improved technology, skills, resources etc. But equally important is to become aware and collectively address various exploitative and discriminatory forms of social evils and issues.

While there are specific procedures on formation of groups, thrift and credit, grading of groups etc., there are no guidelines on social mobilization. It is clear that unless social mobilization is largely a qualitative process; one cannot have a uniform set of rules for this. A social mobilization strategy was implemented by raising awareness, providing information to and communicating with the groups.

After joining the programme, SHG women took up social activities like Immunization, Pulse polio, HIV/AIDS, Hygiene awareness, and monitoring of governmental activities like prohibition, health, ICDs, antiliquor and literacy campaign etc.

Interactive interviews with the SHGs in the rural areas indicate that women at the grassroots level were exposed to this motivational activity through cluster coordinators, animators or facilitators. Women in the villages were approached by health workers.

The following criteria are taken for measuring and evaluating social mobilization.

Table – 5.1

Criteria for measuring social mobilization

S. No.	*Agenda*	*Awareness by Rural SHG members*	*Awareness by Urban SHG members*
1.	Ensuring household food security	54%	42%
2.	Self awareness on reproductive health aspects, awareness and HIV/AIDS.	45%	54%
3.	No child marriages	90%	100%
4.	Helping distressed and destitute women	60%	30%
5.	Eradicating consumption of liquor	60%	40%

Activities under social mobilization

- Formation of community based organizations (SHGs, VOS).
- Establishing gender resource groups to provide trainings and for capacity building.
- Gender resource pool – to provide conceptual understanding and support on regular basis and for constant monitoring.
- Developing a resource base area – to measure a region over a period of time – Maternal Mortality Rate (MMR), Infant Mortality Rate (IMR), Sex ratio, Cases of violence etc are taken care off.

- Established community based support systems like Family Counseling Centers and Day Care Centre etc.

Throughout the district from every habitation SHG women volunteers (8) were selected and trained by Zilla Samakhyas and Mandal Samakhyas.

Social mobilization Process that facilitated good practices

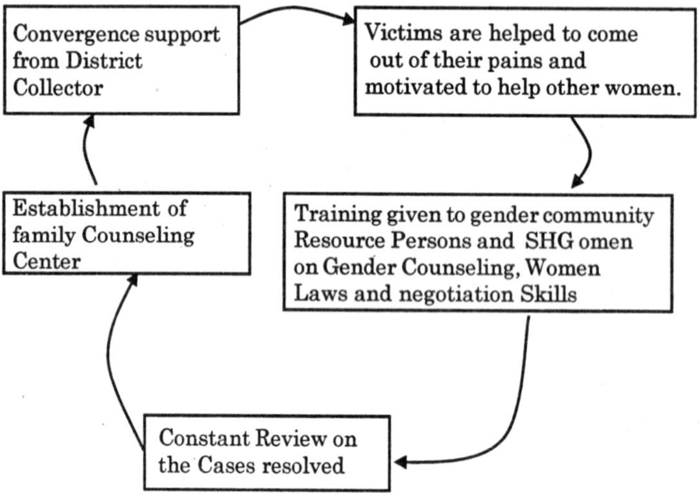

Fig 5.2

Social mobilization plays a vital role in building social cohesion within groups and among institutions. Having achieved scale and voice through federations, they have taken up several problems that effect women on a daily basis and found sustainable solutions to them such as Family counseling centers. A special effort is made to identify the victims of domestic violence, especially among single women and a participatory rehabilitation approach is adopted.

This particular programme adopted Mission Approach. It is a way of scaling up the SHG movement without diluting the objectives and the trust.

The salient features of Mission Approach

- Intensive sensitization and capacity building of various stake-holders is high.
- The sustained groups motivate the un-reached marginalized communities.
- Enable women to develop capacities to demand legitimate services from the various sectors.
- Creates an enabling environment and provide opportunities for decision-making leading towards empowerment of the self and community.
- In Vizianagaram Rural SHGs are built on process as well as activities oriented.
- Out of 80 SHG members in rural areas four persons were selected as community resource persons at the village, two at the Mandal level and one at the district level. Whereas in urban areas from all the four municipalities only four community resource persons were selected. This denotes, from the sample study, strong cadre of community based resource persons are created at the rural areas than in urban areas for nurturing and stabilizing the existing groups.

A conscious effort to focus on social issues such as on girl child, child labour, food security etc., is made by the rural SHGs than urban SHGs. This shows that the cohesiveness among the rural SHG is more when compared to urban SHGs.

Both in rural and urban areas it increased participation, mobility and visibility which led to institution building, thereby building social capital.

In Vizianagaram district, the mobilization and formation of SHG is mostly done by the own functionaries of APOs, MDOs. Grama Sevikas, DRDA (District Rural Development Agency) and

Department of women and child development are the main promoting agencies.

NGOs have been actively involved from the beginning in mobilizing and organizing SHGs and it is observed that more number of NGOs in rural areas when compared to urban areas have spent considerable time and efforts in training their staff on mobilization and organization of the community.

Along with the Government, Banks and NGOs, the community based organizations, the sustained groups, especially in rural areas played a prominent role in the social intermediation processes by forming and nurturing of newer SHGs with the leftover poor, the very poor, the destitute and disabled.

As social mobilization is an ongoing process, the government has to take more care and concern and separate budgetary allocations should be made for institution and capacity building.

Income generating activities

The well-being of people is unquestionably the ultimate object of all development efforts and the basic quest of human endeavour is always to seek a better quality of life. The quality of the life of the citizens of a nation can be effectively improved by raising the standards by living of the people on the street and in the backward areas. Social empowerment in general and women empowerment in particular is very fundamental in achieving this goal. The instinct of democracy provides a strong foundation for harmonizing social and economic objectives. Thus within the broad democratic framework, there are great opportunities for synergizing women and economic growth progress to deliver better quality of life in the shortest span of time (Sengupta and Singh 2001).

Importantly economic empowerment has been considered instrumental for holistic development. In the changed context of rural development, there is clear emphasis on sustainable development and promoting of micro enterprises, which demand microfinance/credit. Interestingly, women's crucial contribution in community development, social change and economic independence is highly stressed by many individuals, institutions and agencies.

Self help movement through savings has been taken up as a mass movement by women. There are about 8.50 lakh women SHGs in Andhra Pradesh covering nearly 111.81 lakh rural poor women. The SHGs are not only resorting but are also taking small loans out of the corpus available with the group. An amount of Rs.4025.55 crores is mobilized as corpus among these groups and the savings of these SHGs have an accumulated savings Rs.1962.50 crores as on Feb. 2009. The State Government has extended financial support to the poor women with low or nil saving capacity and who depend on moneylenders or private sources to meet their expenditure and other obligations. During the group meetings, the thrift amount is pooled and given as loans to members for utilization, production or investment purposes based on priorities determined by the group. The group members keeping in view the interests and prosperity of the member take a collective decision regarding all matters. These groups play the role of a moneylender with the care and concern of a mid-wife. Since it is members thrift that is given out as loans to one or two members at each meeting depending upon the priorities as set by the group, members exercise close supervision on utilization of loans. Peer pressure is extended on members to continue savings to enable every member to have an opportunity to avail loans. Prompt repayment of loans is insisted by the remaining members to avail themselves loans of higher order. As a result, at any given point of time all members in a SHG will not be borrowers. Even if all of them are barrowers, their loan out standings will not be equal. Several interesting features have been observed in the financial dynamics of groups where there is endure in qualitative shifts in loan portfolio in favour of productive purposes as against consumption loans availed earlier. So, is the case with the size of the loan. Thrift and credit activities have thus emerged as solitary binding force to mobilize poor women into group mode. With a view to make thrift and credit activities meaningful for economic empowerment, the groups are gradually encouraged to deploy their funds investment on income generating activities. While doing so, conscious efforts are made by Self Help Promoting Institutions (SHPIs) to build appropriate capacities for managing micro-enterprises. Loan availing through banks meet the immediate needs. However, the loan amounts are so small that the urge of the poor women to start up big units is not met. Similarly larger issues like buying raw products in bulk, production in large quantity, packing, marketing etc., cannot be undertaken by SHGs due to limitation of membership and corpus. Hence A.P. Government took up the task of providing financial assistance by mobilizing loans from banks etc., to overcome the problem.

The development agenda of the State of Andhra Pradesh in the last few years is to extend provision and delivery of credit as a financial service to the poor to take them out of poverty by taking up meaningful and productive action. As this study was conducted at Vizianagaram, the income generation activities taken by rural and urban women are examined and in-depth analysis is done. This is a SHG bank linkage programme and group members availed loans at different levels depending upon their thrift and savings activities.

Some of the salient features of SHG bank linkages programme are:

1. The group should have been in active existence for a minimum six months.
2. The group should have successfully undertaken savings and credit operation from its own resources.
3. Evidence of democratic setup in the group where members have a say in all matters.
4. The group should be maintaining proper accounts/records.
5. The banker should be convinced that the group has come

into existence only for the sake of participation in the project and availing benefits. There should be a genuine need to help each other on work together among the members.

6. The SHG members should preferably have homogeneous background and interest.

7. Any interested NGO or Self Help Promoting Institution (SHPI) concerned should help the SHG by way of training and other support for skill upgradation and proper functioning.

8. To generate livelihood for the poor.

Usually, the first loan of Rs. 50,000 will be for an income generation activity. Once they repay the loan on time they are eligible to borrow a second and bigger amount, then a third and fourth and so on. The more loan they repay, a higher loan amount will be available to them. Various livelihood loans such as for agriculture, animal husbandry etc. are available as they go up the ladder. As the loan amounts increase, so does the borrower's quality of living. At some point the borrowers are able to break out of the threshold of poverty.

Because inflation is still taking its toll, it is putting pressure on poor women whether to repay their debts or meet their daily needs. In general these higher inflationary trends could result in declining funding from low cost savings. So these factors are to be viewed as significant challenges to maintain healthy operation of entrepreneurs and repayments. The new kind of reaction by the poor women to the crisis in their lives is beginning to show that the poor can be efficient under varying socio-economic and political circumstances through their own participatory organizations. They save, invest, create assets and can achieve a high level of human development even at low levels of growth. They begin to assert their right to resources to which they are entitled. Here, the women participate as subjects of development.

Diversified occupations are observed among the respondents in Table 5.1. The micro enterprises taken up by the members in the study area can be broadly classified under the following heads. Agriculture Activities (AA), Animal Husbandry (AH), Food Processing (FDP), Forest Produce (FP), Petty Trades (PT), Services (SE), Skill oriented activities (SK) and Multiple activities (M).

Table – 5.2
Income generating activities

S. No.	*Income Generation Activities*	*Abbreviation*
1.	Agricultural activities	
	a) Sharecropping	AA
	b) Nursery	
2.	Animal Husbandry	
	a) Goat rearing	AH
	b) Milk animals	
3	Food Processing	
	a) Papads	FDP
	b) Pickle Making	
4.	Forest Produce	
	a) Broom sticks	FP
	b) Tamarind	
5.	Petty trades	
	a) Fruits & Vegetables vending	PT
	b) Provisions / Kirana	
6.	Services	
	a) Dhoby	SE
	b) Catering	
7.	Skill oriented	
	a) Weaving	SK
	b) Handicrafts	
8.	Multiple Activities (Poultry, Dairy)	
	a) STD booth	MA
	b) Tailoring,Weaving, Cultivation	

Table 5.3
Distribution of rural, urban SHG samples on the basis of economic activities

S. No	*Economic Activities*	*Number of bene-ficiaries in Rural area*	*%*	*Number of Bene-ficiaries in Urban area*	*%*	*Total No. of members*	*Total %*
1	AA	48	60	04	05	52	32.5
2	AH	02	2.5	01	1.25	03	1.87
3	FDP	04	5.0	12	15	16	10
4	FP	08	10.0	10	12.25	18	11.25
5	PT	04	5.0	18	22.5	22	13.75
6	SE	06	7.5	20	25	26	14.44
7	SK	06	7.5	11	13.75	17	10.62
8	MA	02	2.5	04	5	06	3.75
Grand Total		80	100.0	80	100.0		100.0

Out of all the economic activities in the rural areas maximum number of SHG women (60%) opted for agricultural activities and in urban areas maximum number of SHG women (25%) have chosen services. Under the study area both urban and rural, maximum number have chosen agricultural activity 32.5 percent; 14.44 percent of members are engaged in services, 13.75 percent members engaged in professional trades, 11.2 percent members in food processing and 10.62 percent members opted for skill oriented activities.

Distribution of respondents according to their income generating activities

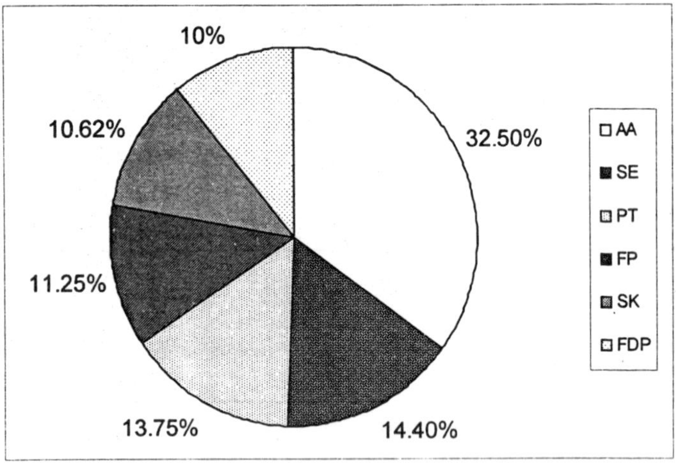

Fig. 5.3

It is interesting to note that in rural areas 72 percent finances have been extended through bank loans for initiating income generating economic activities. The savings made by the SHGs are only 16 percent and community investment find is 12 percent. In the case of urban areas 60 percent of the finances have been extended through bank loans for initiating micro enterprises. The savings made by the SHGs are 22 percent and the community investment fund is 19 percent. When compared to urban areas repeated loans were taken by rural SHG members (13.75%) and in urban area 72.5% of SHG members availed loan at the first level.

After completion of six months of the formation of SHG, first level of loan Rs.50,000/- will be granted by the banks. At the second level Rs.1 lakh to Rs.1.50 lakh will be sanctioned. At the third level members are encouraged to borrow Rs.3 lakh and above depending on the worthiness of repayment of loans.

Table – 5.4
Bank linkages utilized by rural & urban SHG members at different levels

S. No.	*Economic Activity*	*Rural SHG Women*			*Urban SHG Women*		
		L1	*L2*	*L3*	*L1*	*L2*	*L3*
1	AA	24	16	08	03	01	-
2	AH	02	-	-	01	-	-
3	FDP	02	01	01	10	02	-
4	FP	06	01	01	06	02	02
5	PT	04	-	-	12	04	02
6	SE	04	02	-	16	03	01
7	SK	03	02	01	08	02	01
8	MA	01	01	-	02	01	01
	Total	46	23	11	58	15	07

The data relating to the income generation of the rural and urban SHG women was estimated under various economic activities taking in to consideration the income before and after joining programme, percentage of increment is calculated. Again in the same economic activity increment percentage of SHG women both in rural and urban areas availing Bank linkages at different levels was also estimated.

From the above table on an average there is 150 percent increase at the first level in almost all economic activities and there is 210 incremental percentages at the third level. This denotes that definitely at all levels there is an increment in the income levels after joining the programme. In the rural areas those who were engaged in multiple activities, received an increment percentage of 258 and also in the services there is an increment percentage of 255. In the skill oriented trades also there is an increment percentage of 228.

It may be understood that the groups in above activities are sustained groups and availed repeated loans. They possess more skills and expertise in those areas.

Table 5.5

Economic activities taken up by rural SHG women and increment percentage at various levels of Bank Linkages

S. No.	Economic activity	Bank linkages at various levels	No. of women	Total Investment (CIF+ Savings)	Income Before Joining the Program	Income After joining the Program	Interest Repayment	Net Income	Income	Increment %
1		2	3	4	5	6	7	8	9	10
1	AA	L1	24	137280	40128	117120	16473	100647	60519	150.81
		L2	16	183040	34112	21964	21964	87636	53524	156.90
		L3	08	257280	20096	92128	30873	61255	41159	204.81
2	AH	L1	02	11440	3156	8480	1372	7108	3952	125.00
		L2	-	-	-	-	-	-	-	-
		L3	-	-	-	-	-	-	-	-
3	FDP	L1	02	11440	3300	9830	1372	8458	5158	156.00
		L2	01	11440	2165	6920	1372	5548	3383	156.00
		L3	01	32160	2580	11240	3859	7381	4801	186.00

(Contd...)

	1	*2*	*3*	*4*	*5*	*6*	*7*	*8*	*9*	*10*
4	FP	L1	06	34320	10104	30060	4118	25942	15838	156.74
		L2	01	11440	2088	6235	1372	4863	2775	132.00
		L3	01	32160	2546	11210	3859	7351	4805	188.00
5	PT	L1	04	22880	6752	19944	2745	17199	10447	154.72
		L2	-	-	-	-	-	-	-	-
		L3	-	-	-	-	-	-	-	-
6	SE	L1	04	22880	6400	19992	2745	17274	10847	169.00
		L2	02	22880	4380	13940	2745	11195	5615	255.00
		L3	-	-	-	-	-	-	-	-
7	SK	L1	03	17160	4830	14988	2059	12929	8099	167.68
		L2	02	22880	4420	16400	2745	13655	9235	208.90
		L3	01	32160	2756	12916	3859	9057	6301	228.62
8	M	L1	01	5720	1646	5181	686	4495	2849	173.00
		L2	01	11440	2286	9560	1372	8188	5902	258.00
		L3	-	-	-	-	-	-	-	-

Table 5.6

Economic activities taken up by urban SHG women and increment percentage at various levels of bank linkages

S. No.	Economic activity	Bank linkages at various levels	No. of women	Total Investment (CIF+ Savings)	Income Before Joining the Program	Income After joining the Program	Interest Repayment	Net Income	Income	Increment %
	1	2	3	4	5	6	7	8	9	10
1	AA	L1	03	18600	5460	16360	2232	14148	8688	159.12
		L2	01	12400	2480	8210	1488	6722	4242	171.04
		L3	-	-	-	-	-	-	-	-
2	AH	L1	01	6200	1836	5790	744	5046	3210	174.83
		L2	-	-	-	-	-	-	-	-
		L3	-	-	-	-	-	-	-	-
3	FDP	L1	10	62000	18980	61280	74440	53840	34860	183.66
		L2	02	24800	4692	17312	2976	14336	9644	205.54
		L3	-	-	-	-	-	-	-	-

(Contd...)

1		2	3	4	5	6	7	8	9	10
4	FP	L1	06	37200	10920	35280	4464	30816	19896	182.19
		L2	02	24800	4560	16220	2976	13244	8684	190.43
		L3	02	67200	5760	26560	8064	18496	12736	221.11
5	PT	L1	12	74400	22536	73800	8928	64872	42336	187.85
		L2	04	49600	10240	36792	5952	30840	20600	201.17
		L3	02	67200	6480	28596	8064	20532	14052	216.91
6	SE	L1	16	99200	28960	87840	11904	86736	57776	199.50
		L2	03	37200	6630	25415	4464	20951	14321	216.00
		L3	01	33600	2980	13580	4032	9548	6568	220.40
7	SK	L1	08	49600	14480	45824	5952	39872	25392	175.35
		L2	02	24800	4830	20256	2976	17280	12450	257.76
		L3	01	33600	2956	13210	4032	9178	6222	210.48
8	M	L1	02	12400	3728	11780	1488	10292	6564	176.07
		L2	01	12400	2382	9210	1488	7722	5340	224.18
		L3	01	33600	2980	14242	4032	10210	7230	242.61

Out of the 8 economic activities in the urban areas skill oriented economic activities helped women to come out of poverty as the increment percentage is 257.76 and next occupies the multiple activities the increment percentage being 242.61.

Further the characteristics of the rural and urban micro enterprises and markets in Vizianagaram district is represented in the following Table 5.7.

Table 5.7
Characteristics of rural and urban enterprises and markets in vizianagaram district

S. No.	*Characteristics*	*Rural Areas*	*Urban Areas*
1.	Scale of enterprises	Predominantly small	Small, medium and Large
2.	Intermediary providers of inputs and credit services	Few private providers	Many private providers
3.	Public structure and infrastructure	Scarce, unreliable and expensive	Relatively favourable
4.	Markets for products and labour	Highly seasonal	Year round
5.	Access to markets	Poor access to markets	Good access
6.	Competition	Thin markets, many nearly natural monopolies	Most sectors have competitive markets
7.	Transaction cost in markets	High due to poor infrastructure, and many small dispersed buyers and sellers	Relatively low

Most often banks under finance the micro-entrepreneur. What emerges is that starting a micro enterprise is not dependent on one source of funding alone but multiple sources depending upon the type of enterprise and the finances required. However there is a good initiative and spirit in SHG members for starting up income generating activities.

As regards the adequacy of amount in rural areas, 86.25 percent of the members and 91.2 percent members in urban areas, who had availed loans felt that the amount was adequate for the micro enterprise. This is a reasonably good figure. In the rural areas 13.75 percent and in urban areas 7.75 percent were of the opinion that the amount was inadequate. However they could not pinpoint any specific reason for saying so.

Further the amount of loan available and availed by urban SHG women during this period increased substantially. More number of rural women from marginalized communities are able to access loans when compared to urban areas. It is also seen both in rural and urban areas that the government has emerged as a fast self help promoting Institution (SHPI) in Vizianagaram district. Since 2005, government of AP has emerged as a major SHPI when compared to earlier years. However, loans availed by the members of rural areas is quite high when compared to urban areas.

The time taken for getting repeated loans is an important indication of the performance of SHGs. There is a wide variation across the municipalities in the time taken for getting the loan from bank. The co-ordination between the banks and government departments as well as procedural and administrative methods often lead to delays in timely release of loans to the SHGs. Only 51 percent of the respondents in the urban areas, 78 percent of the rural areas said that they have received loan in one month time, whereas 49 percent of the urban and 22 percent of the rural areas SHG members said it has taken them more than 4 months.

When asked about which agency has been the main motivating and supporting factor for starting a micro enterprise about 78 percent from the rural areas named government officials, banks 20% and NGOs 2 percent. In urban areas SHG women motivated to start micro-enterprise by the government is 62 percent and by the banks 38 percent. The umber of members motivated by government is more because it is largely target oriented. Family members in the urban areas are playing a major role giving co-operation and support in running the micro enterprises and in the rural areas family members of the SHGs do not seem to be playing any role. Almost 57.5 percent of the micro-enterprises in the rural areas are initiated by the members of a more than one year standing.

The success or failure of any enterprise depends on multiple factors both at the individual and at the wider level.

The project had two major components

Firstly the awareness campaigns that reached out to 205 SHGs rural and 20 urban SHGs on various technologies for income generation and the second component was training and enterprise building in specific income generating activities for different areas.

Awareness campaigns include the interaction with large number of community based organizers: NGOs and SHGs and executed through posters, pamphlets, demonstrations and short films.

Based on the form the awareness campaigns and interaction with various SHGs, community-based organizations, specific income generation activities were undertaken in the urban areas. In the rural areas income generation activities mostly based on the availability of time and gave less importance to profits.

Capacity building is an effort to develop the following qualities among the women SHGs:

1. skill development
2. ability to plan
3. to decide
4. to organize
5. to carry out activity
6. to deal with people / institution.

Of the respondents who have attended the training, around 68 percent in rural areas and 44 percent in urban areas felt that the training and capacity building has been in tune with the enterprise they have taken up. These figures are much higher in rural areas compared to urban areas. The duration, nature and the methods used in the programmes are quite revealing. Most of the programmes are for 2 – 3 days (80 percent) or at the most about a week (5 percent).

So far as the content of these programmes is concerned most of them are on general awareness, basic orientation etc. Skill development is given much priority in the urban areas. Further practical learning through exposure and interactive methods is not given emphasis in the training module. Although the training input has gone up, most of these trainings are largely informative both in rural and urban areas.

Interestingly when asked about adopting improved methodology of production overall, around ten percent of respondents in the rural areas 12.5 percent in urban areas said, they did introduce some of the methcds. 12 percent for rural areas and 16 percent from the urban areas said that they also received marketing support in this regard.

There are several agencies who are involved in training such as NGOs, MDOs and DRDA officials who are playing a key role in providing training.

Table 5.8
Training programme organized for rural and urban SHGs

S. No	*Name of Training*	*Duration (Days)*	*Members participated*	
			Rural	Urban
1	AA	3 days	48	04
2	AH	3 days	02	01
3	FDP	2 days	04	12
4	FP	7days	08	10
5	PT	2 days	04	18
6	SE	2 days	06	20
7	SK	7 days	06	11
8	M	3 days	02	04

The Mandal Samakhyas and Town level federations are taking certain interventions to enable the rural and urban SHG women to develop their capacity, knowledge skill and managerial aspects in certain economic activities and thereby showing the awareness for income generation in a sustainable manner. The thrust is on providing technical, managerial and marketing skills, required for the development of agriculture and allied sectors in rural areas. Building the capacity of the women SHGs to manage their own activities is a vital component in the entire development approach. Capacity building is a process of enhancing the knowledge, skill and attitude of women SHGs to free future challenges and fulfill social commitments with the help of other actors in the society. It enhances the ability of women to do what is required for them.

The employment created and income generated would vary and is specific to each enterprise. When asked about the additional number of days of employment that the enterprise has been able to generate in a month, about 57 percent of the rural members and 42 percent of the urban members expressed that it has given less than 10 days and 10 percent of rural and 12 percent of urban reported between 11 to 15 days and 37 percent of rural and 36 percent urban respondents said that it has generated 21 or more days of employment slightly over 65 percent in rural and 52 percent of urban respondents feel that the employment generated through their enterprise is sustainable. Overall around 82 percent in rural and 75 percent in urban areas think that the enterprise provides them employment in varying degrees.

Over 36 percent of women from rural areas and 44 percent of women from urban areas feel that they take a reasonable amount of decision-making role in the management of the enterprise. More than 60 percent both in rural and urban areas continue to manage both household and the enterprise. This shows that while the workloads of the women has increased, the support and sharing by the family members is not visible. Almost 60 percent of the respondents in rural areas and 55 percent in the urban areas fee that the enterprise gives them reasonable source of income.

A comparison of the household monthly incomes before taking up micro enterprises and after joining the programme reveals that 32.8 percent members in rural areas and 46 percent in urban areas have moved out from a monthly income of Rs. 2,000 to the next level of Rs. 3,000 – 4,000. One of the possible reasons for this could be that members who possess more skills might have taken advantage of the loans and moved to the next level.

The most visible impact is the reduced dependence on money-lenders as a result of income available from the micro enterprise. This is an encouraging sign and shows that women who are members of SHGs have access to loans from their own savings and groups to meet their immediate consumption and social needs as well as initiating small income generating activities.

6

Empowerment

This chapter throws a light on the importance and evaluation of empowerment and how it is useful in poverty alleviation. Any talk of empowerment does have social, culture and economic under-pinning essentially linked to it. While the very concept of 'empowering women' do vary in terms of space, degree and time, yet societies have been grappling and trying to understand this concept and address issues and meanings attached to it. No doubt this approach do have an anti-women societal notion of women from men's eye and patriarchal mindsets laced to it, are often blamed for marginalizing women for ages.

The key issue here is why we talk of empowerment? The justification could lie on this. Irrespective of too many National and International agreements affirming their human rights, women are still much more likely than men to be poor, malnourished, illiterate and backward. They usually have less access than men to health, property ownership, credit, training and employment. They are far less likely than men to be politically active and more likely to be victims of domestic violence.

In the above scenario women's empowerment is critical to sustainable development and the realization of human rights for one and all. The process of empowerment would mean a shift from sphere of domestic to public sphere (Serdar and Shea, 1990).

It is obvious, that any approach that address and understand women empowerment must address the cultural, social, economic and political issues. Overall empowerment of women has to be viewed from all these parameters vis-à-vis, the background functional and structural backwardness and subjugation of women on all these frontiers. The thrust shall be on whether any micro or macro approach adopted to empower women carries ingredients to uplift women from cultural and social barriers, economic marginalization, from no decision making space to a level of having a say in decision-making and having a wider participation in community level exercise. Women empowerment need not be empowerment *per se*, not as achievement of 'power over' another but the development of what is referred to as "power to, with and from with in" (Afshar, Haleh, ed. 1998).

The recent thrust on women empowerment is on 'income generation'. This particular programme IKP focuses on the need for poor women to earn incomes, making relatively small investments in income generating activities. This programme has been effective in empowering women's economic status because the A.P. government has started with the promise that women are fundamental to the process of economic development.

Women's empowerment is not a one time affair but a continuous process. The impetus may arise out of experience, disadvantage or discrimination or an aspiration to become self-dependent. The empowerment process may be based on an institutional frame work and sustained through input - output exercises. Initial activities may include micro-finance, income generation community education, mutual support, services and advocacy. Empowerment is a process that takes a person from a position of powerless inaction to responsible action. The process moves through several stages from (1) participation to (2) decision-making to (3) action and ultimately to (4) the capacity to take responsibility for those actions.

Empowerment is understood in terms of the capacity of the poor women SHGs to influence development processes, and consequently achieve greater well-being. The evaluation depends on two distinct elements. The first is an explicit causal framework of empowerment itself. The second element is a causal framework for how empowerment influences development. Empowerment has received a rising profile as a source of more effective, and more inclusive development. This is particularly so in the sense of increasing the capacity of poor women SHGs to influence development process. One marker for this was incorporation of empowerment as one of the primary forces for poverty reduction by the World Bank in its Millennium World Development Report (World Bank 2001) and in subsequent strategy statements – and this from an agency more commonly associated in the public mind with market liberalization and technocratic solutions. A subsequent World Bank Publication states that "A growing body of evidence points to the linkages between empowerment and development, effectiveness both at the society-wide level and at the grassroots level (World Bank 2002).

There has been considerable study of the role of empowerment related factors in poverty reduction and overall development. Yet, there are few, if any, rigorous evaluations that allows the contribution of empowerment to be measured, and compared with other influences on developmental outcomes, whether at the local or society-wide level. There is also paucity of empirical analysis on causal influences on empowerment itself. Yet, this type of information is crucial for public action that is intended to foster empowerment relative to other pressing concerns of policy makers and other development agents. This involve a variety of mechanisms, including interventions that promote participation, increase transparency, build capacity amongst poor women SHG groups and strengthening accountability mechanisms.

By empowerment we mean increasing the capacity of the groups to make purposeful and effective choices in the interest of pursing a better life for themselves. This can be applied to any group, but chiefly concerned with the empowerment of poorer, excluded or subordinate groups, and the analysis may be developed from that perspective. There are, unsurprisingly multiple definitions of empowerment in its related literature that emphasize different aspects of the concepts.

The empowerment of women is becoming an increasingly popular term in human rights and development discourses and by development agencies. This chapter examines what does empowerment really mean and how does one know when a programme like this has been successful i.e. How it has succeeded in empowering women? This study looks at various definitions of empowerment and how to measure it. When empowerment of women is stated as a goal it is important to be able to measure the progress and hence to identify what works and what does not in different contexts.

Defining Empowerment

The many different definitions of empowerment in use show that it is an elusive concept and that defining it is difficult. Rappaport has said that "Empowerment is like obscenity, you don't know how to define it but you know it when you see it". Most definitions of empowerment include concepts such as agency, self-reliance ability to make choices and awareness etc.

According to Adams (1996), "Empowerment is the means by which individuals, groups and communities to take control of their circumstances and achieve their own goals, thereby being able to work towards helping themselves and others to maximize the quality of their lives. Dubhashi (1997) considered empowerment as exercising control over ones lives, firstly on resources of financial, physical and human and secondly on beliefs, values and attitudes.

The *Social Work Dictionary* (Barker, 1991), defines empowerment as "the process of helping a group or community to achieve political influence or relevant legal authority".

According to Zippy (1995), empowerment represents "a means for accomplishing community development tasks and can be conceptualized as involving two key elements giving community members the authority to make decisions and choices and facilitating the development of the knowledge and resources necessary to exercise these choices".

According to Pillai, J.K. (1995), "Empowerment is an active, multidimensional process which enables women to realize their full identity and powers in all spheres of life. Power is not commodity to be transacted; nor can it be given away as aims. "Power has to be acquired and once acquired, it needs to be exercised, sustained and preserved."

According to Bandura (1986), "Empowerment is the process through which individuals gain efficacy, defined as the degree to which an individual perceives that he or she controls his or her environment."

While discussing empowerment Jo Rowlands (1997) has identified four different forms of powers.

- Power over—control or influence over others which is an instrumentation of domination;
- Power to—generative or productive power which creates new possibilities and actions without domination;
- Power with—a sense of the whole being greater than the sum of the individuals, especially when a group tackles problems together;
- Power from within—the spiritual strength and uniqueness that resides in each one of us and makes us truly human. Its basis is self-acceptance and self-respect which extend, in turn, respect for and acceptance of others as equals.

Though the interpretation 'Power to' and 'Power with' empowerment is concerned with the process by which people become aware of their interests and how those relates to the interests of others but also participates in decision-making and influence such decisions.

Stromquist (1995), in her article on educational empowerment tor women, interprets empowerment as a "socio-political concept that goes beyond formal political participation and consciousness raising. She argues that a full definition of empowerment must include cognitive, psychological, political and economic components". She explains that:

- The cognitive component refers to women having an understanding of the conditions and causes of their subordination at micro and macro levels. It involves making choices that may go against cultural expectations and norms;
- The economic component requires that women have access to and control over productive resources, thus ensuring some degree of financial autonomy. However, she notes that changes in the economic balance of power do not necessarily alter traditional gender roles or norms;
- The political entails that women have the capability to analyse, organise and mobilise for social change; and
- The psychological component includes the belief that women can act at personal and social levels to improve their individual realities and the society in which they live.

Stromquist notes that there is general agreement that these components are interrelated.

Garba(1999) argued that the enhancement of women's capacity to influence and participate in decisions that directly or indirectly affect their lives, is a key issue in raising their standard of living and protecting their rights to full participation in the process of development. In other words, empowering women is a means to an end, the end being to improve their lives and protect their rights to participate in decisions that affect them.

Karl(1995) offers a useful framework for identifying enabling conditions for the process of empowering women; awareness, participation, capacity building and decision-making. Hazel Johnson (1992) looking more specifically women's empowerment in the context of the increase in women's organisation and collective activities ėmphasise gaining a voice, having mobility and establishing public presence with improved economic independence and self-confidence.

Naila Kabeer (1994) emphasises the importance of such elements as self-respect and the sense of agency in empowerment processes and also the building of organisational capacity through conscious processes, support for leadership development and strengthening of networks. There is strong focus on the collective dimension as an adjunct of personal empowerment.

Empowerment as a process of a community or a group there of gaining autonomy and control over one's life. As a result of the empowerment, the empowered should become agents of their own development, exercising choices, selecting their own agenda and changing their status in the society. In the context of gender and development, empowerment should be viewed more as a process than as an end product. It is a dynamic process changing according to circumstances. It applies to the individual as well as the collective. At the individual level, empowerment involves building up the self-image and self-confidence as well as the critical faculties to think, decide and act. On a collective plan, empowerment means enabling women collectively to take control of their own lives, to set, their own agenda, to organise each other and make demands on the state and the society for change.

Yet, in spite of the diversity of approaches, a recent survey found a "greater consensus .... On its conceptualization than expected (Malhotra et al. 2002 p.4). It is found that the terms most often in its definition are: options, choice, control and power. Naila Kabeer, for example, asserts that empowerment is "the expansion in peoples ability to make strategic choices in a context where this ability is previously denied to them" (Kabeer 1999, p.437). This definition highlights both the actors' ability to make choices and the process of change in the achievement of these abilities. She emphasized the need to examine a poor group's resources, agency and achievements in interpreting the process of empowerment.

In the World Bank source of book on empowerment, Deepa Narayan states that empowerment is the expansion of assets and capabilities of poor women to participate in, negotiate with, influence, control and hold accountable institutions that affect their lives (World Bank 2002 b, pxviii for other recent work on the nature of empowerment with in the World Bank see Bennet 2002 and World Bank 2002 C). Like Kabeer's, this definition highlights that empowerment refers to the actor's ability to make purposeful choices and that it involves a process of change. It also emphasizes that empowerment is about the transformation of those choices into actions and that this is a function of the institutions with which poor women SHGs interact. (The ability to make purposeful choices is usually referred in the literature as the agency component of actors. More on this see Giddens 1984, Sen 1985, Emirbayer and Mishee 1998).

This study considers empowerment as a compounded concept that involves both the capacity of the individuals and groups to make purposeful choices (that is to be agents), and the ability to transform these capacities for agency into favourable outcomes via interactions within the social and institutional context in which actors live. It may be said that there has been empowerment when poor groups exercise agency with a reasonable prospect of this having an influence on development process and outcomes. Whether the priority lies for empowerment lies in strengthening the capacities of the poor groups or making the institutional context more respective will depend on the initial conditions.

Empowerment can have value for intrinsic and instrumental reasons. Having more power over one's life is valued for its own sake in almost all societies, and it is important to recognize this intrinsic value of increased choice or empowerment (Sen 1985, 1992). But empowerment is also potentially of importance for its impact on other aspects of development – for its influence on the process that led to less income poverty, lower morality, greater skills and less insecurity. Such capacities to influence development occur with in a world of multiple other causes. The development process is complex, and – as a large quantity of development study has sought to document – a whole range of factors are germane to the realization of such development outcomes. These factors include public spending on education, health and micro credit etc.

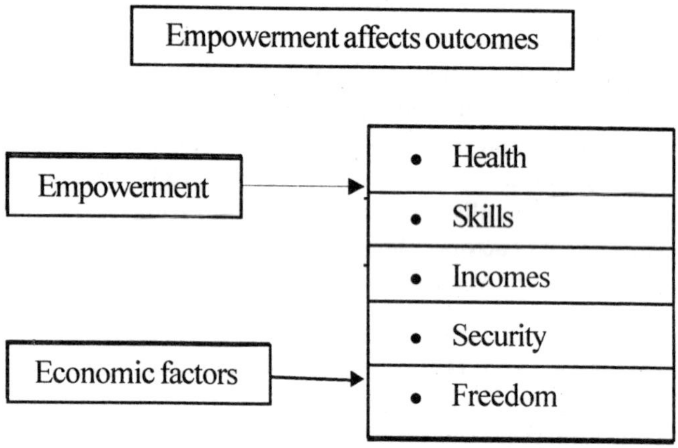

Fig 6.1: Diagrammatic Representation of Empowerment

Thus in evaluating empowerment, great stress is needed in outcomes for the poor, and subsequently an independent account of the empowerment process is also required which will allow assessment of causal relationships with development outcomes with in the context of the multiple influences on the development process. Evaluating the role of empowerment involves question of how to attribute changes to empowerment-related changes, whether these involve increased capacities of the disempowered groups or changes in the context that allow existing groups to be more effective. This is an example of common, indeed a classical, question in evaluating the causes of development process. It may be viewed here that empowerment is compounded concept: a product of interaction between the agency, capacities of the poor groups, and the context in which these can potentially be exercised. The agency capacities of individual groups are the products of a range of influences, including their economic resources, human capital and individual capacities, but also capacities that flow to a significant context from their socio-cultural background. The extent to which agency can be effectively exercised depends on the context, that determines the structure of the opportunities faced by individuals and groups. This opportunity structure is a product of formal rules, informal socio-cultural structures, the power and strategy of other groups. [This can be seen as an extended version of synthesis of resource mobilization, political opportunities and cultural approaches with the social movement literature *see* Tarrow (1998) for general discussion.]

In fine, empowerment is of intrinsic positive value for those who become more empowered. This can often bring benefits in terms of greater aggregate production, efficiency or well-being in a society. But it is by no means necessarily the case that instrumental influences are beneficial to all. For empowerment of poor groups will often lead to the relative disempowerment of previously dominant groups. Hence, empowerment need to be harmonious, and may lead to heightened conflict or other outcomes that at least some groups would judge in a negative light. This is a matter for both causal and normative analysis.

In this empirical work, the hypothesis is that empowering poor SHGs can lead to changes in the development in ways that may increase outcomes such as health, educations and incomes. The influence and behaviour of poorer SHGs does not occur with in a vacuum, but rather within a system in which many other influences are at work.

Participatory engagement may often be a feature of empowerment, but is by no means the only means by which poor SHGs may be able to exert greater influence. Socioeconomic, political and institutional factors also have an influence both on decision making and on the extent to which poor SHGs are empowered.

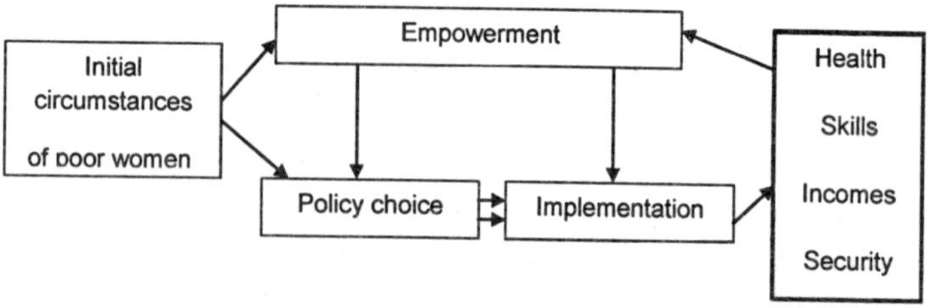

Fig 6.2: Empowerment Process

Empowerment is the instrumental sense of affecting development process (such as decision-making or service delivery), only makes sense in the context of an interaction between poor SHGs and others. There are varieties of forms of interactions, including voting, sharing information etc. Empowerment is only about a subset of these interactions, involving the expression of preferences via 'voice' in order to change the socio-cultural norms and practices.

Women's Empowerment Indicators through Microfinance

- Ability to save and access to loans.
- Opportunity to undertake an economic activity.
- Mobility-opportunity to visit near by towns.
- Awareness – local issues, microfinance institutions procedures, banking transactions.
- Skills for income generation.
- Decision making within the house.
- Group mobilization in support of individual clients action on social issues.
- Role in community development activities.

Source: Impact Assessment, Frances Sinha (2003).

In this particular study on disadvantaged communities especially women are offered new hope through forming into Self Help Groups. Micro-finance increases women's economic spaces when interventions provide access to credit, financial service and product. It is a means for income generation and increases abilities to build and own assets. Microfinance thus has the potential for economic empowerment. Economic empowerment through micro-finance most often makes positive shifts in physical spaces, since women have to become more mobile and need to have better control over their bodies and labour. Economic empowerment most often makes positive shifts in political spaces, especially for women, in collective mobilization when they hold positions of authority and leadership and learn to share information in groups.

Women empowerment can be viewed as a continuum of several interrelated and mutually reinforcing components (Marille, Karl 1995).

They are:

- Awareness building about women's situation, discrimination and rights and opportunities as a step towards gender equality. Collective awareness building provides a sense of group identity and the power of working as a group.
- Capacity building and skill development, especially the ability to plan, make decisions, organize, manage and carryout activities to deal with people and institutions in the world around them.
- Participation and greater control and decision-making power in the home, community and society.
- Economic independence.

Based on the components of empowerment, and the nature of the respondents questions were formulated in the question form, where the respondent was required to answer in terms of totally agree, agree, cant say, disagree.

Based on the preliminary exercise, a scale was developed consisting of 80 items. In some questions sub-questions were also provided which were for all practical purposes counted as a single item. Thus a preliminary scale was prepared to ensure proper evaluation of empowerment.

The pre-testing of the empowerment scale was done through individual interview method to a group of 40 in rural and 40 in urban areas. Based on the preliminary responses, the following criteria, was used for selection of items. The items which have brought forth a particular response (positive or negative) from the majority of the respondents were not considered as diagnostic in differentiating the level of empowerment. Care was taken to see that all the items were scored in one direction, and it was done in the positive direction. Such of those items, which were negatively toned, are reversed in scoring. Finally 48 items were selected distributing the items across the different characteristics of empowerment.

In order to examine the relevance of the items that constitute empowerment, correlations were worked out between awareness and participation. The correlations were significant at 1 percent level. These two variables are important prerequisites for providing information base for setting a path for empowerment process.

In order to establish relationship between information empowerment variables and identified economic variables like economic independence, and capacity building correlation matrix was calculated. The correlations were significant at 1 percent level except economic independence which is significant at 4 percent level.

The formal score therefore consists of 48 items, each item was required to be answered in terms of totally agree, agree, can't say, disagree, with a score of 4-3-2-1. The analysis was done separately for economic and non economic variables of empowerment. The total score of each component was calculated and for the sake of better understanding the scores were conducted in to percentages.

Awareness and participation are interlinked and it is the first step in the process of empowerment. Awareness among the rural SHG women is quite high (84 percent) and in urban SHGs it is 72 percent, the reason for this predominance in rural areas may be that SHG concept was known to them since two decades and this is a newly introduced concept at urban areas.

It is observed that majority of the women (85 percent) in rural areas participated quite actively in their SHGs in attending meetings, operating savings, and credit and the participation of urban SHG women is comparatively low (78 percent). Overall the participation level across the district is good.

Further empowerment is measured by degree of economic independence and capacity building. Regarding economic independence in terms of having the freedom and control over money earned and its use, mixed results are obtained from the respondents activities.

One of the dimensions of women empowerment is the decision-making capacity and the ability to influence members with in the family. Being in SHGs and having access to credit and starting economic enterprises has given power to make decisions at the household level both in rural and urban areas. After joining the scheme, SHG women gained more confidence, visibility and more access to credit. This in turn has paved a way for political empowerment also. In rural areas active participation of women in Grama Sabhas, and micro level plans was found. In the urban areas too they have succeeded in implementing environment protection by totally abandoning polythene bags.

Overall the study reveals that the process of empowerment has already set in among the SHG members both in rural and urban areas. Thus the empowerment of women through SHGs led to gain benefits not only to the individual woman but also to the families and community as a whole through collective action for empowerment.

Qualitative empowerment from economic, social, political and psychological perspectives is also examined.

It enabled the women both in rural and urban areas to earn their livelihoods, besides participating in the process of development. It may be observed that rural women's participation is more in income generation activities when compared to urban women. Urban women used micro-finance more for their consumption purposes than for entrepreneurial purposes. Hence, it may be stated that rural women SHGs are good examples of capacity building for prospective entrepreneurs. The SHGs in rural areas motivated other women with no educational or industrial or entrepreneurial back ground to become self dependent and self reliant by developing and enhancing the decision making capacity of members, installing in them confidence to solve heir problems. It has provided a forum to learn about mobilizing collectively money and financial matters.

It has also increased the awareness levels about the society and community. Through this group approach, they started participating voluntarily in campaign against eradication of social evils like dowry, child marriages, family counselings etc.

Women's political participation is now recognized universally as a crucial element in augmenting the cost effectiveness of any plan for socio-economic progress. During the field survey 75 percent of the members in rural areas stated that they are taking active participation in the political process by attending Grama Sabhas and raised their voice for their needs. The women in urban areas were also active in approaching the ward counselors and expressed their grievances. Further, a SHG woman from Iddanavalasa village was elected as Sarpanch also. Thus experiences in Vizianagaram district shows that the leadership in SHGs may serve as a gateway to more active participation and empowerment.

The status of women is intimately connected with their economic position, which in turn depends on opportunities for women in participating in economic activities. In this study it is found that investment in income generating activities improved their livelihoods with in the household and outside as well on an average both in rural and urban areas there is a raise in monthly income ranging from Rs.1, 500 to Rs.2,000 after joining the IKP. It is obvious that the returns from the economic activity are used not only for women's welfare but also for the welfare of their children and family and the community at large.

Social interaction is reported to be much better among the members after joining the groups. This is a gradual process, which would take place only when the functioning of the group becomes sustainable. The extent of empowerment varies with the age of the group. Members in rural SHGs showed a high degree of social and psychological empowerment than their urban counterparts.

Further, SHGs have not only produced tangible assets and improved living conditions of their members, but also helped in changing much of their social outlook and attributes. The group dynamics have reasonably helped the respondents to overcome the feeling of low esteem and lack of confidence and empowered them psychologically. For measuring the social impact of SHG members, a three-point scale consisting of high, medium and low was used to assess empowerment based on members responses and general observation. It is given in Table 6.1.

Table 6.1

Members perceptions in psychological empowerment in rural and urban areas

Factors	*In Rural Areas (%)*				*In Urban Areas (%)*			
	High	*Medium*	*Low*	*Total*	*High*	*Medium*	*Low*	*Total*
Self confidence	38 (43.75)	35 (47.5)	08 (10)	80	38 (43.75)	35 (43.75)	07 (8.75)	80
Community skills	25 (31.25)	46 (57.5)	09 (11.25)	80	42 (52.5)	28 (35)	10 (12.5)	80
Mutual help & cooperation	68 (85)	10 (12.5)	02 (2.5)	80	46 (57.5)	22 (27.5)	12 (15)	80
Attitudinal change	21 (26.25)	42 (52.5)	17 (21.25)	80	25 (31.25)	36 (45)	19 (23.75)	80

In rural areas because of their homogeneity and group affiliation, mutual trust, cooperation is more (85 percent). Self-confidence levels were also increased reasonably. On the whole both in rural and urban areas, there is a perceptible change in their behaviour, attitudes and communication skills also.

Most importantly gender equity and equality was also examined. Their attitude both in rural and urban areas has been impressive. A gradual shift in women's perception about the girl child is a clear sign of their changing attitude.

7

Impact, Impressions and Suggestions

The self help approach is found to be a successful instrument for combating poverty in a sustainable way. It focused on improving the quality of life for marginalized women. In this study it is observed that both in rural and urban areas wherever SHGs were formed they worked with group dynamism for common interests and for mutual benefits. The SHG strategy empowered the women socially and economically to live a life of dignity with their children in their community and they were able to overcome all social, economic, cultural and psychological barriers through their self-managed organization. It has enabled the disadvantageous and marginalized women to perceive possibilities for change and thus brought about a desired change through their collective action. SHGs have inculcated the savings habit among the poor women. However there is no aggregate data about SHG savings. Certainly through this programme, the poor women got an identity, access to information and bargaining power. It has provided a platform for the poor women to discuss and resolve their own problems. It enabled the members to manage cash flow deficits maintaining food intake and overcoming emergencies which led to improvement in quality and productivity of their own capital/resource – human capital / resources. They were able to come out of the clutches of the private moneylenders to some extent and learnt the art of asset creation and diversification their occupations. It is understood from the study, given a chance, the poor women have adequate potential sparks which can be well fanned in to flames with necessary guidance and training through SHGs, thereby bringing them to live on par with men in all spheres of human life in our society. SHGs have effectively implemented a number of programmes of donors, official agencies, and civil society organizations, for example, the vast network of federations were implementing pension distributing programmes, managing mid-day meal programme at schools and working on awareness building for health, legal issues, HIV/AIDS, child labour etc. It is evident that SHG federations were seen by the government as an alternative channel for service delivery of governmental programmes.

The programme supported the Government in procurement and marketing services, Non Pesticide Management, rice credit line activities, preparation and implementation of annual work and finance plans by linking different schemes and programmes.

Further it has also strengthened micro-financial services through bank linkage and institution building through community resource persons strategy. It enabled to identify good SHG members who have come out of poverty as community resource persons. These CRPs are available to other clusters and thus a good social capital was built around these institutions to get involved in developmental activities in the areas.

The poor have much in common with each other wherever they live. Nevertheless, rural areas around the world share a number of characteristics that are distinctly different from urban areas. Hence, this empirical study examined the specific approaches required to address the needs of the rural and urban poor women separately for a comparative analysis. Rural and urban areas are inextricably linked in the process of development; and the strategy must take into account the diverse range of interactions between rural and urban economies, when creating future developmental efforts. This programme is a statewide poverty reduction project which enabled the poor women to improve their livelihood and quality of life through their own organizations.

Overall, owing to the creation of SHGs, poverty levels in A.P. have declined from 29.75 percent in 1983 to 10.85 percent in 2004-05. Under this programme Indira Kranthi Padham (IKP), in A.P State rural SHGs are working under Society for Elimination of Rural Poverty SERP and urban SHGs are working under Mission for Eradication of Poverty in Municipal Areas (MEPMA) and followed SHG federation strategy to promote SHGs.

Socioeconomic profile of SHG members

- Majority of SHG members belong to poor socio-economic strata both in rural as well as urban areas.
- Members belonging to the SC community form a high proportion in rural areas (37 percent) and a high presence of members from Backward Classes (B.Cs) is found in urban areas (50 percent).
- With regard to the religion it is found that Hindus predominated both in the rural (92.60 percent) and urban (90.01 percent) areas under the study.
- The families were mainly of the small sized nuclear type (1-4 members), reflecting the national trend. However even in rural areas the nuclear families are (67.88 percent) less than the urban areas (86.72 percent).
- The majority of the members belonged to the age group of 26-40 in rural areas (58.90 percent) and in urban areas (47.82 percent).
- Income-wise (97.5 percent) from the rural areas and (92.46 percent) from the urban areas were below the poverty line.

Thrift and credit activities of the SHGs

- Majority of the members stated that they formed as a group mainly to initiative income generation activities.

- In the study area both for rural and urban SHGs, the foremost motivational factor was thrift and access to bank credit.
- The quantum saved was greater in urban areas than in the rural areas. The monthly savings ranged from Rs.30 – Rs.50 per head.
- It is interesting to note that 90 percent of the respondents both in rural and urban areas said that the amount used for savings is from their own earnings / sources.
- The majority of the groups both in rural and urban areas reached 100 percent level of savings, which is highly remarkable.
- It appeared that income from their own labour was the main source towards their thrift contribution.
- Savings to the tune of Rs.3,43,600 was mobilized from 20 urban SHGs in contrast Rs.2,64,840 was mobilized by the 20 rural SHGs. The amount saved by an individual SHG was in proportion to the number of members and the duration of their functions.
- In the rural areas, SHGs are more matured (3 to 5 years) when compared to Urban SHGs (3 years). Because of their maturity, there is a perceptible shift in utilizing the loan amounts from consumption to product needs. In both the areas bulk income is used for income generating activities which in turn provided employment and income to the members.
- Majority of the women from rural and urban areas had benefited out of the internal lending, the loan amounts varying from Rs.1,000 to Rs.2,000.
- The loan repayment behaviour was satisfactory. In the rural areas the recovery index was 90 – 100 percent for five SHGs and 80 – 90 percent for twelve groups and in the case of

urban areas the recovery index 80 – 90 percent for six SHGs and remaining SHGs full under 60 – 80 percent.

Group characteristics

An attempt has been made to analyse the cohesiveness among the rural and urban SHGs by taking into account the contributing factors like group cohesion, group interaction, group leadership transparency, need satisfaction, interdependency of members, team spirit accountability, group co-operation and equity. The study revealed that the majority of respondents (85 percent) of rural areas were in the higher category for variables such as group cohesion, group leadership interdependence of members, team spirit and group co-operation, while the variables need satisfaction, accountability and equity. Majority of the respondents 77 percent in the urban areas fall under the medium category. The difference in the level of group cohesiveness across the rural and urban areas is significant. It could be due to various factors such homogeneity/heterogeneity, quality of capacity building, leadership styles and different types of activities taken up by groups. Co-operation in terms of meeting, helping each other and sharing responsibilities among rural and urban SHGs is quite positive.

Social mobilization

The aim of social mobilization is to unleash innate abilities. Social mobilization is not automatic. It is to be induced. The programme show the process of social mobilization as an institutional mechanism to facilitate the poor to interact with government machinery, so that public resources and services are better utilized. It is important to account for the social capital which is generated in the process of social mobilization when SHGs are formed. In rural areas mobilization of more uncovered and un-reached marginalized communities was done by older groups through motivation. This is relatively low in the case of urban areas. It is found that the impact of social mobilization – organizing the poor is obvious and glaring in the case of rural areas through community resource persons.

Capacity building

Both in rural and urban areas it has contributed to self-reliance by encouraging the requisition of relevant skills and development of supportive structures and institutions. It includes the aspects of training, consultancy, personal development and mentoring. Out of the total sample of 160 only 64 members have attended training in rural areas and 55 members in the urban areas.

Entrepreneurialism

It is often discussed as the lynchpin to sustainability and empowerment. It is linked to income generation and development initiatives. Entrepreneurial skills are equipped more in the case of urban SHG women than in rural areas.

In the study area, net working of rural SHGs at the Panchayat level and urban SHGs at the urban local bodies helped to achieve some economic goals of the groups.

Group dynamics

Rural SHGs are homogenous whereas urban SHGs are heterogeneous. But with regard to the collection of savings both rural and urban SHGs are doing well. All the SHGs both rural and urban areas had become aware of bank procedures.

The qualitative gains as revealed by 160 women, both in rural and urban areas indicated that women were in the process of attaining various attributes of empowerment which would bear testimony to the positive outcomes of economic independence acquired by women through undertaking micro enterprises and it is proved that the women are really becoming partners of development.

Awareness generation on health, education, education of children is quite high both in rural and urban areas.

Awareness, participation and mobility are high among the rural SHGs 84 percent and in urban SHGs it is 72 percent.

Being in SHGs and having access to credit and starting economic enterprises has given power to make decisions at household level, particularly in education, health care etc.

Self perception of SHG member is high in the case of rural areas when compared to urban areas. It gave them more confidence, visibility, access to credit which in turn has altered the way they are perceived by their own families, community and banks etc.

Before joining the scheme both rural and urban women earned less than Rs.1000 per month and now their income is increased after joining the programme and they were able to earn around Rs.4,000. But due to inflation, there is hike in prices and thus this too may be a meager amount but certainly useful for their sustenance.

Suggestions

Based on the findings of the study, the following suggestions and recommendations are made in the interest of the welfare of the women in general.

- Emphasis should be not on sanctioning of units, but on growing the units.
- Timely release of funds is extremely important for implementation of the programme and delivery of benefits to the poor women.
- DRDA/ Government agency should send timely proposals for release of second and third installments.
- It should be mandatory to DRDA's to spend an amount of Rs.5 lakh annually towards management of professional input related to marketing research, value addition or product diversification, which would facilitate marketing of the produce of the poor women.
- There is a need to improve marketing, including expansion of fairs at multiple places.

- The groups need to adopt and nurture internal systems that promote transparency and accountability. These should go beyond book-keeping and audit to governance, communication etc.
- To become effective demand groups they need to learn through experience, to influence external resource institutions and stakeholders.
- Need to introduce debt swapping modality to come out of the debt trap of private money lenders. The debt swapping will be a one time measure to extend additional loan to repay their existing loans to private lenders.
- Need to recognize SHG women not as beneficiaries of some schemes or programmes but to treat them as primary stakeholders in the process of development.
- Coordinated approach should be followed by better functioning of SHGs with three major components namely women's empowerment, capacity building and access to inputs as well as technology and other resources.
- There is a need to establish a separate credit bureau. A credit bureau is a system where client's credit information is collected from lenders and maintained.
- Need to provide unique identity number at the earliest.
- NGS in tribal areas should be encouraged at all levels with sufficient financial grants, appreciation and awards.
- Conducive atmosphere and harmonious network should be established among government agencies, banks and NGOs for effective functioning of the SHGs to avoid overlapping and duplication.
- Banks should work with open mind to promote SHGs among women, particularly among the downtrodden community like SCs, STs in order to bring them into the mainstream.

- Special attention on group development in urban areas i.e., participation, contribution, democracy, mutual help and solidarity, relationship across levels should be developed.

- Government should play a facilitating role; not a target oriented one and restrain from enlarging the agenda of SHGs.

- There is need for decentralized capacity building and support services and for every 5 – 10 SHGs, there must be a mentor emerging from the movement itself.

- Follow up activity need to be done, so that the problems could be attended to spontaneously. In the absence of such mechanism, women feel left out and helpless.

A distant outcome of the programme is that large number of women have come out of the confines of their traditional roles and socially circumscribed identities and are playing community leadership roles and engaging with external agencies like banks and government departments. Inclusion of the poor and deliberate efforts to do so does standout in the programme as does the breadth of out reach. Even the poorest have got loans as well as benefits under various welfare programmes. It is a pathway to women empowerment highlighting the need to improve individual and collective capacity and self esteem so that women feel valued and can contribute.

In nutshell, it may be concluded that the SHG strategy is undoubtedly a positive and purposeful experiment for women empowerment in Vizianagaram district, as it opened up floodgates of opportunities to enhance capacities in their development and growth in totality.

Bibliography

Reports

Asian Development Bank 1999, *Key Indicators of Developing Asian and Pacific countries 1999*, vol. 30, Annual Statistical Publication of ADB, Oxford, New York.

A.D.B. Report 2004: *Women SHGs Urban their role in Slum Clearance and Sanitation.*

A.D.B Annual Report 2004, *Special Theme: The changing face of the Microfinance Industry*, MANILA.

Afro Asian Rural Development Organization (AARDO) (2006), "Report of the International Workshop on Empowerment of Women through rural enterprises", held on 20 – 27th March 2006, Hyderabad.

Andhra Pradesh Statistical Abstracts, Directorate of Economics and Statistics. Government of Andhra Pradesh, Hyderabad 1995.

Annual Report, 2004 – 2005, NABARD, Mumbai.

Census of India, 2001.

Chief Planning Officer, *Hand Book of Statistics*, Vizianagaram District, 2005 – 2008.

Comprehensive Poverty Eradication through Social Mobilization and Empowerment of Rural poor women, Report by T.

Vijayakumar and Rajasekhar (2008), SERP, Department of Rural Development, Government of Andhra Pradesh.

Department of Women and Child Development, Fourth World Conference on Women, *Country Paper*, 1994, Beijing, New Delhi, 1995 p. 4.

Five Year Plan Documents 1952 – 2002.

Eleventh Five Year Plan, Government of India, New Delhi, 2007–2012.

Human Development Report 2007, A.P. Centre for Economic and Social Studies, Nallakunta, Hyderabad.

IMF Review (2005) PRSPs indicates Microfinance as Key Component.

Sadhan – 2004: A study on SHG – Bank Linkages and status of MFI in Bihar BASICS Ltd ., (Bharatiya Samrudhi Investments and Consulting Services Ltd., Ranchi, April 2007 (Final Report).

Shramashakthi: *Report of the National Commission of Self Employed Women in the Informal Sector*, Department of Women and Child Development, 1998.

Tankha, Ajay 1999 : "Some NGO Dilemmas in Reaching the Poorest with Microfinance". *Search Bulletin* 14(1) : 73-79.

UNDP- *Human Development Report 1990*, New York; Oxford University Press.

United Nations Development Programme (UNDP), *Annual Report: Enduring Poverty and Building Peace through Sustainable Human Development*, New York : 1996 – 1997.

Women's Self Help Groups in Andhra Pradesh – Participatory Alleviation in Action (2004) Report by Joy Deshmukh – Ranadive, Centre for Women's Development Studies, New Delhi.

World Bank 1997 - Achievement and Challenges in Reducing Poverty.

World Bank (2000a). World Development Report 2000/01: Poverty and Development. Oxford University Press.

World Bank (2000 b). *Bolivia: From Patronage to a professional State*. Bolivia Institutional and Governance Review. Washington D.C: World Bank Report No.20115-BO.

World Bank (2001). *World Development Report, Gender and Poverty in India*, OUP, New Delhi.

World Bank (2001), *Engendering Development: Through Gender Equality in Rights, resources, and voice – Summary*. (World Bank.

World Bank (2002). *Review of the Poverty Reduction Strategy Paper* (PRSP).

World Bank (2002 b) pxviii. For other recent work on the nature of empowerment with in the World Bank.

World Bank (2002 b). Empowerment and Poverty Reduction. A source book. The World Bank

World Bank(2003). *Reacting the Rural Poor – A Renewed Strategy for Rural Development*, Washington D.C.

Books

Adams, Robert (1996), *Social Work and Empowerment*, McMillan Hampshire.

Afshar, Haleh, Ed (1998) *Women and Empowerment: Illustrations from Third World*, Basingstoke. MacMillan, 1998.

Agarwal, Anurag (2008), "Micro Finance, Poverty reduction and women" in Agarwal, Babita, *Indian Women – A giant power*, ADB Publishers, Jaipur.

Ahmed, Rais (2008), "Role of Micro Finance in Empowering Women" in Sinha, Ajit Kumar, (ed). *New Dimension of Women Empowerment,* Deep and Deep Publications, New Delhi pp. 232-267.

Bandura (1986), *Social Foundation of Thought and Action*, Eagle Wood Cliffs, N.J.; Prentice - Hall.

Bennett, Lynn, (2002), *Improving pro-poor growth through greater Empowerment and Social Inclusion: A Social Development approach to analysis and action*, Draft World Bank.

Brody, Alyson et al. (Ed.)(2006), *Managing the Social Performance of Micro-Finance. vol.2* of Money with a Mission London:" Intermediate Technology Development Group of North America, 2006. pp.189.

Chambers, R. (1996) *Relaxed and Participatory appraisal, Notes of Practical approaches and Methods*: Brighton: Institute of Development Studies.

Christsabell, P.J. (2009), *Women Empowerment through capacitybuilding the role of Microfinance*, Concepts Publishing Company, New Delhi.

Consultative Group to Assist the Poorest (CGAP) (2003), Focus Note No.24, Washington, DC.

Copestake James (2006) et al. (Eds.) "Micro Finance and poverty reduction." vol. 1 of money with a mission. London: Intermediate Technology Development Group of North America, pp. 253.

Das, Sabyasachi (2005), "Self Help Group and Micro-credit Synergic Integration" in Verma SB and Pawar, Y.T (ed), *Rural Empowerment through SHGs, NGOs and PRJs*, Deep and Deep Publications, Delhi pp 27-37.

Deepa Narayan (2005), *Measuring Empowerment : Cross Disciplinary perspectives*, World Bank, 2005.

Dev, S. Mahendra (2006), "Inclusive growth in India : Performance, issues and challenges," First Dr. P.R. Dubasi Lecture, 2006, Gokhale Institute of Policies and Economics, Nov. 29th, 2007.

Deve, H.R. 2007. *Commercial aspects of SHG Banking in India, NABARD,* Mumbai.

Dubhashi, P.R, (1997) *Micro Finance and Empowerment of SC's Women, An impact of SHGs*, New Delhi.

Fisher, T. and Sriram, M.S. (2002), *Beyond micro-credit: Putting development back into microfinance*, New Delhi: Vistaar Publications.

Frances Sinha – Access, use and contribution of Micro finance in India: Findings from a National Study (2005) Frances Sinha (2003), Impact assessment.

Frances Sinha, Ajay Tankha et al. (2006), *SHGs in India, A study of the lights and shades*, EDA Rural Systems in Association with A.P. Mahilabhivrudhi Society, Hyderabad.

Giddens, Anthony (1984). *The constitution of Society, Outline of the theory of structuration*, Cambridge: Polity Press.

Goel, Aruna (2004). *Organization and Structure of Women Development*, Deep and Deep Publications, New Delhi.

Hashemi, Syed M and Sidney Ruth Schuler (1993). "Defining and studying empowerment."

Hemalatha Prasad, C (2006), "Social mobilization, Employment and Empowerment of Women through SHGs", National Institution of Rural Development, Rajendra Nagar, Hyderabad.

Jerinabi, U, *Micro Credit Management by Women's Self Help Groups*, Discovery Publishing House, New Delhi.

Kabeer, Nailer (1994), *Empowerment of Women – Conceptual Framework*, The World bank, Washington DC.

Kabeer, Nailer (1999). "Resources Agency, Reflections on the measurement of women's empowerment", Development and change, 30(3): 435 – 464.

Kropp, E.W, (2002) "A Review of the Progress and Impact of the Overall Strategy for scaling up the SHG - Bank Linkage Programme Over the last decade.

Little field, E. and Rosenberg, R (2004), 'Micro-finance and the poor: Breaking down walls between micro finance and formal finance, *Finance and Development*, 41(2): 38-40.

Malhotra, A., Schuler, S.R. and Boender, C (2002) *Measuring Women's Empowerment as a variable in International Development* (Washington, DC, The World Bank)

Manjudevi, K (1997), *Rural Women: Poverty Alleviation*, Anmol Publications, Delhi.

Marille, Karl, (1995), *Women and Empowerment : Participation and Decision – Making*, London, Zed Books.

Moser, Caroline (1996) Confronting crisis: A comparative study of Household responses to poverty and vulnerability in Four Poor Urban Communities (Washington, DC: The World Bank).

Narashimha Raju, AV (2008), "Self Help Groups and Women Empowerment", Deep and Deep Publications, New Delhi pp-468-475.

Nath, Vikas 2001, *Empowerment and Governance through information and communication technologies: Women's perspective*, Academic Press, St. Louis.

Nayar K.R. et al. (1985) "Self help: what future role in health care for low and middle income countries?" (http://www.equityhealthi.com) *International journal for equity in health* 2004, 3:1 doi: 10, 1186/1475 – 9276 - 3 - 1, 2004,15th April.

Osman, Khalil, "Micro Finance Institutions: Effective weapon in the War against Rural Poverty", www.muslimedia.com.

Peter Sullivan, Vice President, Asian Development Bank. *ADB review*, Vol.31, No.3, 1999.

Pillai, JK (1995), *Women and Empowerment*, Gyan Publishing House, New Delhi.

Puhazhendhi, V & Badatya, K.C. (2002) *SHG Bank Linkage Programme for Rural Poor in India, An Impact Assessment*, NABARD, Mumbai.

Purushotham, P (2005), "Marketing Support to the SHGs", in rural empowerment though SHGs, NGOs and PRIs", Ed by Verma, S.B and Pawar, Y.T, Deep and Deep Publications, New Delhi, pp 1-15.

Razi, Shahin (2007), *Rural Development and Voluntary Organizations, Classical Publishing*, New Delhi.

Rangarajan, C. (2006), *Micro finance and its future directions.*

Rao, R.S, et al. (2006), *Fifty Years of Andhra Pradesh 1956 – 2006*, Centre for Documentation, Research and Communication, Hyderabad.

Reema Nanavathi (2000), *Women Work and Poverty*, SEWA, Ahmedabad.

Remenyi, J., & Quinones, B (Ed.) (2000) *Microfinance and Poverty Alleviation: Case studies from Asia and Pacific*, Pinter, London.

Rhyne, E (2001) *Mainstreaming Microfinance*, Kumarian Press, Connecticut, USA.

Ritu Jain et al. (2007) "Socioeconomic impact through Self Help Groups", in Verma, S.B and Pawar, Y.J., *Rural empowerment*, Deep and Deep Publications, New Delhi, 2007.

Rowlands, Joe (1996) "Measuring Empowerment : Cross disciplinary, perspectives", The World Bank, Washington DC.

Sahu and Tripathy (2005), "Self Help Groups and Women Empowerment", Anmol Publications, New Delhi.

Sen, Amartya K. 1985 a. Commodities and capabilities. Amsterdem: Elsevier.

Sen, Amartya K. 1992, *Inequality Reconsidered*, Cambridge, Mass: Harvard University Press.

Sen, Amartya K. (1999), *Development as Freedom*, New York: Alfred A. Knopf.

Seibal and Dev, H.R. "Study on SHG Bank Linkage in India – *Working Paper* –9.

Sidney, R., Hashemi, S.M. and Riley, A., (1997), 'The influence of women's changing roles and status in Bangladesh's fertility transition: Evidence from a study of credit programme and contraceptive use', *World Development*, 25(4):563-5-75.

Sinha, Ajitkumar (2002). *Dynamics of Poverty Alleviation Programmes*, Deep and Deep Publications, New Delhi.

Singh, Kavaljit, Banking sector Liberalization in India: Some distributing trends, *ASED*, August 29, 2005.

Singh, Sitaram (2005). *Poverty Alleviation in Third World*, APH Publishing Corporation, Delhi.

Stromquist, Nelly P. (1995). "The theoretical and Practical Bases for Empowerment : Women Education and Empowerment : Pathways towards Autonomy", UNICEF, 1994.

Subrahmanyam, P.V.V, (2006) *Rural Women and Self Help Group Strategy*, Andhra University, Visakhapatnam.

Tarrow, Sidney. 1996 "States and Opportunities: The Political Structuring of Social Movements" in McAdam, Douglous, Mc Carthy, John and Zald Mayer, 1996."

Tarrow, Sidney 1998. *Power in Movement. Social Movements and Contentions Politics*. Cambridge: Cambridge University Press.

Tendulkar, S.P (1998) *India's Economic Policy, Reforms and Development*. Essays for Man Mohan Singh, OUP, New Delhi.

T. Sai K.S., (2004), "Imperfect Substitutes: The Local Political Economy of Informal Finance and Micro Finance in Rural China and India", *World Development*, 32(9) : 1487-1507.

Journals

Barker, R.L. (1991). "The Politics of Social Empowerment", *Social Work*, vol. 4, No.2.

Berik, G Ü n Seli and Vander, Yana, (2009), "Feminist Economics of Inequality, Development and growth", *Feminist Economics*, vol.15, No.3, July, Houston, USA., pp.1-33.

Das Gupta, R. (2005), "Micro credit summit campaign", Washington, DC. vol.1, Issue 4: May /June 1998.

Das, Sabyasachi (2005), "Self Help Group and Micro-credit Synergic Integration" in Verma SB and Pawar, Y.T, (ed.) *Rural Empowerment through SHGs, NGOs and PRJs*, Deep and Deep Publications, Delhi, pp. 27-37.

Elson, Diane (2009), "Gender equality and Economic Growth in the World Bank, World Development Report 2006", *Feminist Economics*, vol.15, No.3, July, Houston, USA pp 35-59.

Emir bayer M and Mische Ann. (1998) "What is agency?" *American Journal of Sociology*. vol.103 (4)

Garba, Kassey P (1999). An endogenous empowerment strategy: a case study of Nigerian Women, *Development in Practice*, Vol. 9, No. 1 and 2, Feb. 1999.

George, N.D. (2008), "Micro Finance Issue and Strategies", *Yojana*, Jan. 2008, pp 41-43.

Kabeer, Nailer (1999). "Resources Agency, Reflections on the measurement of women's empowerment", *Development and Change*, 30(3): 435 – 464.

Mallick, Anupriyo (2007), "Social Mobilization: An empowering tool for community development," *Kurukshetra*, Aug. 2007, pp22-25.

Nayar K.R. et al. (1985) "Self help: what future role in health care for low and middle income countries?" (http://

www.equityhealthi.com) International journal for equity in health 2004, 3:1 doi: 10, 1186/1475 – 9276 - 3 - 1, 2004,15th April.

Patil D.A., Dheer A.M. (2009). "ICT and Women Empowerment of Rural and Deprived women, *Asia - Pacific Journal of Rural Development,* Centre on Integrated Rural Development for Asia and Pacific, vol. XIS, No.1, July, 2009.

Reema Nanavathi (2008), "Micro Finance approach towards Livelihood Security", *Yojana,* 2008.pp. 21 -23.

Sankaran, P.N (2004), "Rural Urban Development – A Partnership Perspective", Kurukshetra, Vol. 53, No.2, Decembêr 16-19.

Satpathy, Asuthosh (2008) "Women's Empowerment in India – SHGs, Micro-finance and Technology experiences", *Tech monitor,* March-April 2008, pp. 34-43.

Sen, Amartya K. (1985) b. "Well-being, Agency and Freedom. The Dewey Lectures 1984". *The Journal of Philosophy,* Vol. LXXXII No.4.

Serdar, B and Schwartz - Shea P (1990). "Empowering women: Self: Autonomy, and Responsibility." *The Western Political Quarterly,* 44(3): 605-624.

Shylendra, H.S. (2008), "Role of Self Help Groups", *Yojana,* Jan. 2008, pp 25-28.

Sinha, Frances (2005), "Access, use and contribution of Micro Finance in India: Findings from a National Study", *Economic and Political Weekly,* April. 23.

Swarna Sadasivam, Vepa (2008), "Technology adoption and micro-finance: Micro-enterprises run by women in India", *Tech Monitor,* March-April, pp. 17-24.

Yerram Raju, B (2008), "Micro Finance development and Regulation", *Yojana,* Jan. 2008, pp. 31-35.

Zippy Allison (1995). "The Politics of Empowerment, *Social Work*, vol.4, No.2, March, 1995.

Web Sites

http://www.nabard.org/roles/microfinance.

http://www.undp.org/women/mainstream/undp.shtml

http://www.rd.ap.gov.in/velugu/veluguactionplans/mf.htm

http://poverty.suite101.com/article.cfm/feminization_of_poverty#ixzzofd7qpb56.

www.rd.ap.gov.in/ikp/ikp_process_jan_2010.

www.worldbank,org/gender/prr/engerndersummary.pdf.

Index

■■■